THE ENTREPRENEURS

Volume One

Elizabeth Hennessy

SCOPE BOOKS

First impression February 1980

© Scope Books 1980
3 Sandford House, Kingsclere,
Newbury, Berkshire RG15 8PA

British Library Cataloguing in Publication Data

Hennessy, Elizabeth
    The entrepreneurs.
    Vol. 1
    1. Businessmen — Great Britain — Case studies
    2. Entrepreneur — Case studies
    I. Title
    338'.04'0941   HC256.6

    ISBN 0-906619-02-5
    ISBN 0-906619-03-3 Pbk

Printed in England
Signland Limited, Farnham, Surrey

PUBLISHER'S FOREWORD

This book is the forerunner of a series entitled "The Entrepreneurs" to be published throughout 1980 and 1981. The author of this first volume, Elizabeth Hennessy, has spent six months researching and writing.

John Ferguson, ARCA, FRSA, has designed this book and its cover.

We are indebted to Raymond Monbiot for his vigorous and enthusiastic introduction which follows. It explains better than we can, why this book is being published. Incidentally, Mr Monbiot, the Managing Director of a large public company, has also written for us our next book, "How to Manage Your Boss", a brilliant, satirical and psychological study addressed to all executives in business and other fields.

The Publisher, John M. Ryan

INTRODUCTION

For those who appreciate achievement and enterprise this book will provide a stimulating and enjoyable read. Set out is the story of four men who have each developed the ability to identify a market need and satisfy it. What is more, as their businesses have grown through their efforts, they have managed to keep in touch with consumers and their changing tastes. The remoteness, normally associated with large companies, has not been allowed to intervene, even though there are many thousands of people working for their respective enterprises.

The thread which runs through these four stories of drive and determination, is the willingness to listen. This applies as much to the staff on the ground floor as it does to the management. It shows an interest in ideas no matter where they originate, and very often the stimulus for change comes from those closest to the action. Accessibility and discipline in working habits, which enables those who want or need to talk, to do so, cuts down the distance from the point of decision. Managers are tempted to build empires and retain them to underpin their own status. Indeed, the system of reward used in much of industry is geared to the number of staff and costs you have under you. Ideas which challenge the organisational structure are less likely to come from those who depend upon it, than from those who see it getting in the way of satisfying a market need. For the man at the top to be in touch with the front line is becoming a rare event in big business. Such remoteness and identification with those who keep the business going leaves a gap for an entrepreneur to enter an industry, already the preserve of the giants, and shake it up. This book has many good examples.

Another strength which each of the four has developed and used is the courage to discard. It is one thing to perceive that events have moved on, making what you have obsolete. It is another to have the courage to do something about it, and act. The bigger the company and the longer it has pursued a particular direction, the more difficult it is to change. Positions are defended and change becomes a threat. To the entrepreneur, change is the vehicle he has ridden to success, and he has no plans to step off.

Businesses go through phases of maturity. Many start with a proprietor/manager at the helm and as they grow they develop more functional structures, with layers of management increasing, and complexity breaking down decision making to salaried managers. Overall direction remains in the hands of those at the top, but the means of turning policy into action is delegated. The top down / bottom up conflict is more likely to develop where the original entrepreneur has been replaced by organisational men.

Big business develops its own inertia with a hierarchy, committees and its own institutions formalising decision making, slowing up the action and passing the buck. Plans are built up from below and go through a process of evaluation and discussion which can anaesthetise creative thinking about what the business ought to be doing in a changing environment. Decisions taken from above on an intuitive basis challenge the 'science' being practised by the 'professionals' below and can meet resistance, delay or discouragement.

In such an environment, it can be irritating and frustrating for the managers who are pursuing plans in a qualified and methodical way to be jerked into a new direction by the boss who has a hunch. The entrepreneur builds a special sort of organisation. He has ideas and is powerfully keen to back them with money, energy and action. If he is right he will have several million pounds to prove his record. Try to put an entrepreneur in charge of a more formal and structured business and there will be chaos. He will feel hedged in by 'pedestrian people' who just cannot seem to see the blindingly obvious. They will feel demoralised because at any moment their painstaking work can be overturned as a new direction is indicated.

The atmosphere which an entrepreneur builds around his flair for identifying and satisfying the needs of the consumer is a very special one. A team, hand picked over the years, to compliment his strengths and support his weaknesses will be in tune with the signals. There will be a sense of dynamic pursuit of clear goals which no system can interrupt. The intuitive flair of the boss will be a factor they will admire and rely on, even though they might mutter and grumble at times as their own views are trampled none too gently. The boss's wake is the proof of his competence, and the source of their prosperity. His path ahead is the confident security for their future. The frustrating idiosyncrasies of the boss himself are part of the scene on the way to the objective. Life would be duller and certainly poorer without it.

The picking of a few key people is a skill which enables the entrepreneur to leave in his wake a maturing business as he tackles the next stage of development. The trust with which he delegates a part of his enterprise will determine how his management grow and mature with him. The key members of the team have to be able to get things done as agreed, and develop their own teams in the process, with an expectancy of order and continuity. They must also be willing to be stimulated and challenged at any time by the boss. This is no job for weak and subservient characters. It is no role for any prima donnas either. Many of the best teams are made up of the entrepreneur and one or more associates with whom he has known small beginnings and hard times, where there has been danger and excitement, great hopes and inevitable frustrations.

The entrepreneur believes in money and, as he is motivated by it, he can understand its powerful influence over his team. Elaborate reward schemes so beloved of institutionalised businesses and based on benchmarks of other people's salaries find less attraction to the entrepreneur. His view is more likely to be to share his profit with those who helped him achieve it. A piece of the action for wholehearted dedication to the profit objectives of the business is a straightforward deal. There has to be profit. The business is not a mission dedicated to some non-monetary idealism. It is an unashamed, capitalist enterprise which creates wealth, jobs and progress.

The punishing workload willingly shouldered by these four entrepreneurs has behind it a rock-like determination not to be discouraged. All have faced extreme difficulty, if not actual disaster, at times. Yet events which would have caused lesser men to give up and take a steady job, have fuelled their determination and tenacity and produced new heights of achievement from which to grow further.

This unshakable determination and faith in an idea is infectious to the team that grows around the leader. The pressure on him is then to retain the drive and dedication of that team through good times and bad. If he is worried, then he must never appear to be rattled. If he has doubts, then he must never be doubted. The leader carries the banner through every kind of opposition or difficulty, and that takes courage and character.

No man makes it to the heights of these four without having some very special qualities of bigness, as well as imagination. To hold a team together for years, to retain the cutting edge, calls for an unusual blend of qualities. Such men are rare. Business and society needs them for the enrichment of the consumers' choice. If it were not for the consumers, they would not have succeeded. The consumers, that is all of us, are the richer because our interests have been identified and our needs met.

As you read this book it stirs the blood and sets the adrenalin flowing. These are stories of winners who have won because they had good and relevant ideas, and refused to be losers.

Raymond Monbiot

SIR CHARLES FORTE
Caterer Extraordinary

Sir Charles Forte made a three-minute personal 'telecast', thanking all his staff for their help in achieving record profits over the past year. This was in February 1979 at the introduction of a new TV advertising campaign for his company Trusthouse Forte; the largest hotel, catering and leisure group in the world. Not the expected action of a top British executive, but entirely typical of the kindly, punctilious considerate and polite Sir Charles. "I hate that phrase, the two sides of industry", he says, "industry is all one and this company is one".

The history of the Forte family over the last century is a romantic one filled with dramatic incident which would furnish half a dozen novels. Coming from a small village on a mountain halfway between Rome and Naples, called Mortale, the Fortes had prospered as local landowners, farmers and suppliers of horses to the Neapolitan army. The kidnapping of Constantino Forte by brigands in 1870 during the stormy period of the unification of Italy struck a terrible financial blow to the family who had to raise 38,000 ducats as a ransom. This they succeeded in doing by selling almost all they possessed and borrowing the rest from a rich neighbouring family. One by one the Fortes began to leave Mortale to find work overseas from where they sent back money until all the debts were repaid.

Many of the family went to Scotland in the wake of Pacifico Forte who, after a spell of shopkeeping near Dundee, opened a small cafe selling ice cream (made from a recipe given him by a French chef working in a Dundee hotel – *not* an Italian formula!) Rocco Forte, father of Sir Charles, emigrated to Pittsburgh in the United States and became foreman of an iron works, returning to Mortale to marry and raise a family of five children, one of whom died at birth. Rocco then emigrated again, this time to Scotland; Charles, the eldest surviving child, was sent over to join him at the age of five, in 1913.

Rocco, starting with a small family loan, opened a succession of cafes in his turn, buying and selling, each one a little better than the last. He then acquired a small hotel at Alva, began to make money and was able to educate his son privately, first at Alloa Academy, then at St Joseph's College in Dumfries, a Roman Catholic boarding school; but the boy was homesick for his brothers and sisters and at the age of twelve and a half was sent back to Italy and went to school in Rome. "I had to make a decision at the age of seventeen – university, perhaps in Glasgow – or start work? I decided to work; my ambition then was to build a business as big as my father's, or bigger", recalls Sir Charles.

By this time his father had moved to England and was running a string of cafes and restaurants on the south coast; Forte started work in one of them at Weston-super-Mare and recalls putting in eighteen hour days from 8 a.m. until 2 a.m. Later he moved to Weymouth where he managed two restaurants owned by his father, but the itch to set up on his own was growing, and the opportunity came when he met Eric Hartwell – who is still with him today as Chief Executive of Trusthouse Forte. Hartwell was selling a freezer to Forte senior in Brighton, and thinking of opening a milk bar himself in Worthing with a £1,500 legacy, but Charles Forte suggested they should go into partnership and start up in London.

Charles Forte, now 26, had managed to save some money, every penny of which he put into his new venture, a milk bar in Regent Street. The site was chosen with care: he stood outside the empty shop and counted the number of passers-by with a stop-watch in his hand, evidently coming to the conclusion – it was near the BBC and next door to a cinema – that they were numerous enough to provide a good flow of customers. Just as the importance of the site has been a prime consideration in all his business ventures, so his flair for publicity was demonstrated on this first occasion. The Meadow Milk Bar was opened by the famous Sabu the Elephant Boy, glad of the chance to advertise his film.

To the Meadow Milk Bar the young partners applied a strict budget formula which Forte had worked out and without which, he believes, he might be controlling only a limited operation today. They took a figure as a likely amount for takings and estimated gross profits, wages, rent and other expenses, as well as deciding the minimum sales needed to make it viable. As further premises were bought and added to the group under the name of Strand Milk Bars, (there wasn't one actually in the Strand, but it proved a good name) the same simple but effective system was used as a yardstick to compare one unit with another by means of percentages and ratios. Forte knew the chain he was in process of forming "wasn't my destiny", but was a step on the way towards it. He concentrated on making each one a success before starting the next, and then found he was obliged to learn another skill – the art of delegation – which became more and more important as his business grew larger. He put a manageress into Regent Street when he opened up his second bar nearby in Leicester Square, and was taken aback to find it continued to flourish in his absence.

By the time war broke out in 1939, Forte had nine separate establishments in the heart of London, and had also branched out into catering supplies by opening premises in Percy Street where cakes and fruit syrups could be made and sandwiches cut in one central place, saving him some 20 per cent on his buying costs. Not only did the war put a sudden stop to the expansion, it was also the occasion of a painful incident in Forte's life which it took years for him to get over. When Mussolini joined the enemy Axis he, along with other 'aliens', was interned briefly on the Isle of Man. While branding this action as one of "vengeance and vindictiveness" he has never let it destroy his exuberant patriotism and love for Britain (the Union Jack flies proudly outside some of his luxury hotels in Europe and the U.S.)

3

Meanwhile, Eric Hartwell was in the Army, but in 1946 the Forte operations once more got under way. Hartwell after being demobbed set to work to re-establish and re-equip such premises as had been war-damaged — no easy task in a period of acute shortage — and the two partners who had formed the nucleus of the business were joined by others — Charles' sister Anna and brother Michael, Leonard Rosso, a former Lyons employee on the catering side, and Rex Henshall who supervised acquisitions.

Sir Charles introducing Eric Hartwell (left) to Michael Dickson, Manager of the Albany Hotel, Glasgow

The first of these was Rainbow Corner just off Piccadilly Circus, which Forte bought from Lyons with £30,000 borrowed from the Prudential Insurance Company. He leased part of the building to himself at a rent of £4,000 per annum and let the remainder to the Canadian government for a further £8,000 per annum. Four years later he bought the Criterion site on Piccadilly, for £800,000, which included the famous Marble Hall. The whole site was redeveloped as a banqueting hall. "It was a very satisfactory deal, carried out after a great deal of time, thought and patience". By this time the Forte catering business was firmly enough established to be awarded fifty per cent of the catering contract for the Festival of Britain, held on the South Bank of the River Thames around the still extant Festival Hall. Eric Hartwell has recalled the nights without sleep which both he and Forte spent in their efforts to ensure the success of this, their first venture into the mass market: in contrast to the firm responsible for the other half of the concession, to whom it was, apparently, just a routine operation. The following year, Forte made his first takeover bid for Slaters and Bodega with financial backing this time from the Ind Coope brewery.

"My most glamorous deal" is how Sir Charles describes his next major purchase, the Cafe Royal in Regent Street. He bought it in 1954 and admits that of all his many acquisitions this is the one which gave him the most pleasure. A highly cultured man, who appreciates painting, the theatre, literature and fine arts generally (his office in Park Lane next to the Grosvenor House Hotel which is part of his empire, is decorated with fine paintings and sculpture from his private collection) he had often, as a young man, gone to the Cafe Royal for a sandwich and a lager, "all I could afford". He loved the atmosphere of this famous London landmark where George Bernard Shaw, Arnold Bennett, Oscar Wilde, A.E. Housman and Augustus John had all been regular patrons, but never imagined that one day his company would own it, and even have its headquarters there for a time. Today, over the famous Grill Room and Le Relais restaurant, there are twenty banqueting rooms which can accommodate over 2,500 people. Another central acquisition at about this time, (he was beginning to be known as 'Mr Piccadilly') was the Monico site. He bought the lease, and Jack Cotton the property developer who owned the head lease, paid him £460,000 for it, which Forte put towards his first hotel, the Waldorf.

The Waldorf cost £600,000 in 1958, and not long ago he turned down an offer of £2.5 million for it. Admitting that at the time he knew very little about hotel management, but a good deal about controls and catering, Forte realised this was a turning point in his company fortunes. It was a freehold site in the centre of London, a rare opportunity at that time;

he had enough money, and he had *some* hotel experience in his father's sixteen bedroom hotel in Alva, in Scotland, which also comprised a pub and restaurant. The general manager of the Waldorf was John Lee, to whom Forte has paid generous tribute as the man who taught him the hotel business. Much the same management techniques applied, he found, as had been so successful in his restaurants.

The catering side of the Forte business had expanded enormously during the 1950s. The growth of air transport and early indications of the increase in the numbers of both holiday and business travellers by air were quickly noticed by Forte, and in 1955 his company was awarded the first ever catering concession at Heathrow Airport. They started at Heathrow with one 5-cwt truck. Today Trusthouse Forte Airport Services have 200 commercial trucks, and they service Gatwick, Manchester, Glasgow, Birmingham and thirteen other main airports in the U.K., providing flight catering for seventy-five airlines. They also operate in Europe at, among others, Schiphol in Amsterdam, Orly in Paris (where a 2,000 square metre commissariat supplies the needs of scheduled and inclusive tour airline operators) and West Berlin's Tegel airport.

Alongside airline catering, whose operations are described more fully later on, went a development which has brought Sir Charles more criticism than any other — motorway service areas. He has been involved in these since the opening of Britain's first motorway, the M1 in 1959, when Fortes were appointed to the Newport Pagnell service area in Buckingham-shire. Since then they have added eight more and have become the major caterers in the U.K. network of 1,000 miles of motorway so far completed. Everyone has their favourite motorway food horror story; what does Sir Charles feel about such criticism? He has avowed his intention not to withdraw from these roadside cafeterias, with their unique problems, but rather to concentrate on improving them; and of criticism in general he says philosophically, "it depends whether it's justified or not. If it is, do something about it. If it's not — ignore it". For his part he feels it essential that any criticism he makes should be "factual and constructive".

Sir Charles' move to go public in 1962 was the fruit, he

says, of at least five or six years' careful thought. "We were hesitant, but I became convinced it was the best thing to do, and so it has proved. We couldn't have continued to extend as we wanted to if we had not floated at that juncture; we couldn't have raised money so easily". A certain amount of diversification followed, including entering the entertainments field. Sir Charles has, however, taken care that no Forte venture should in any way be connected with the sleazier side of night life; refusing to put on nude shows at The Talk of The Town which he bought at this point, or to buy any gambling casinos. He also closed down a bar which had become the haunt of prostitutes, ("they have a perfect right to live, but not off me", he has been quoted as saying) even though it was making a handsome profit. Other acquisitions which followed his becoming a public company were piers, inns including the two hundred year old Heneky's Group, the Excelsior Hotel at London Airport and Frederick Group of hotels. It was, by now, a very large company indeed.

Simultaneously, Fortes had been keeping an eye on the possibilities of expanding its catering interests. The group bought Terry's of York, the two hundred-year-old chocolate making firm (although this has since been sold at a good profit) and Ring and Brymer, founded in 1690, which has an impressive record of contracts including the Lord Mayor's Banquet, with which it has been associated for two hundred and fifty years. Ring and Brymer has also catered for such events as the Farnborough and Paris Air Shows, the Chelsea Flower Show and the British Open Golf Championships, and Sir Charles was particularly gratified when they were chosen to cater for the Queen's Silver Jubilee luncheon at the Guildhall in 1977.

In May, 1970, Forte Holdings Ltd. was merged with Trust Houses Ltd., the British hotel chain founded in 1903 to restore the standards of former coaching inns, many of which had become badly run down since the advent of the railways. This took Fortes into the top level of hotel management and gave the group added strength, but paradoxically it also led to the toughest business battle Charles Forte has ever fought. At the time of the merger it was agreed that Lord Crowther, then chairman of Trust Houses, would vacate the top post in a year's time so Charles Forte could replace him. However, there was no shortage of rivals for the job, and shortly afterwards Allied Breweries, made a bid for the merged group which Forte was determined to fight with all his considerable resources. Nonetheless he had to borrow heavily in order to buy Trust Houses Forte shares, which he succeeded in securing to himself, his family and friends to the tune of some £12.5 million, gaining control of 28 per cent; this proved enough to stave off Allied Breweries' bid, which was ultimately withdrawn on January 3rd 1972. Another six and a half years, however, were to pass before the brewers offered their holding, now valued at £48 million, for sale on the stock market − it was snapped up within three hours − and the Forte family have since reduced their own holding to something in the region of 20 per cent.

Like many mergers, this one took some years to work out satisfactorily, partly because the management styles of the two constituent groups were diametrically opposed; one young and forward looking, the other more old-fashioned and leisurely. In an interview with the New York Times in the Spring of 1979 Sir Charles looked back on the turbulent times immediately after the merger and placed much of the blame on the refusal of the Trust Houses element to "listen to me and my management formula". The merger could have worked well, he feels, but in practice the group was "bureaucratically overloaded, a company where memoranda floated backwards and forwards, where people did not communate. I'm a great believer in keeping the bureaucratic element to a minimum. I think it kills initiative, defeats imagination and is a recipe for disaster in both a company and a country".

In the same year as the Trust Houses merger, Charles Forte was knighted. This was not a political honour, but a recognition of his considerable contributions to charity, especially a handsome donation to the newly founded art gallery at Christ Church, Oxford. The Group is currently making charitable grants of between £50,000 and £60,000 a year to such relevant causes as the Catering Trade Benevolent Fund, and additional sums on occasion to the Conservative Party. This is on top of the distribution of income from the 130,000 Trust Shares which is also put to charitable purposes. The eight members of the Group's Council, headed by the Rt. Hon. Hugh Astor, are the Trustees of these shares, which entitles them to the same number of shares on a poll as all the holders of other shares in the company, giving them sufficient voting power to ensure the objects for which the company was formed are upheld.

By the late 1960s the group decided to build on its success in Britain by establishing hotels overseas, and it proceeded to do so, on its own and in some cases in conjunction with British European Airways and B.O.A.C. — now British Airways — with whom the association continues in various joint ventures. Within a few years the group had hotel operations in holiday resorts all round the world from Miami to Sri Lanka, but they were particularly keen to crack the lucrative U.S. market; with sound reason as this has become its biggest source of profit growth. The first American venture was the purchase of the TraveLodge International company in 1973, and the acquisition of this California based corporation added four hundred and sixty hotels and motels throughout North America and Mexico to the Trusthouse Forte operation at one stroke. They followed this up a few months later by buying the renowned Pierre Hotel in New York, which was currently losing $500,000 a year — it now makes $2 million.

In 1977 two master coups were pulled off, firstly the purchase of thirty-five Strand Hotels belonging to J. Lyons for the sum of £27.6 million. Lyons needed cash, and Trusthouse Forte needed hotel bedrooms in the centre of London; through this deal they acquired 3,500 in London and 2,000 more in the provinces. Altogether, at a cost of around £4,000 a room (a fraction of what it would cost to build the equivalent number of rooms in new hotels) they secured the Cumberland Hotel at Marble Arch, the Strand Palace and the biggest hotel in Europe, the Regent Palace Hotel with 1,068 rooms. A fourth hotel at London airport also came in the package, plus the Albany Hotels in Birmingham, Glasgow and Nottingham and the Royal Hibernian in Dublin. Lyons needed the money to pay off heavy interest on the sums they had invested in their catering side, and Trusthouse Forte paid out £7 million for the hotels with the balance to be paid over five years at 5 per cent. Within nine months they looked set to show a profit of more than £5 million a year, and doubled it in 1978, so they are now paying for themselves. "A superb deal" is how it has been described in the City of London, where the carefully planned progressive building up of the group's interests, is closely watched by financial experts and consultants in the hotel and catering fields. It also pleased Sir Charles himself, not only because of its profitability (and the Cumberland is now one of the most profitable hotels in the entire group) but becuase it helped Lyons as well. J. Lyons was itself bought by Allied Breweris in September 1978. They had been unable to find a buyer for the hotels before Trusthouse Forte took on the deal, and Sir Charles describes the whole negotiation as "gentlemanly" on both sides.

The next deal was across the Atlantic once more, when Trusthouse Forte bought up a run down New York hotel chain, the Knott Hotels Corporation; 1,500 rooms this time, in four hotels including the International at Kennedy Airport, the Westbury Hotels in Manhattan and Mayfair, as well as the catering concession for the U.N. Building. Eighty-eight restaurants in the Colony Kitchen group in the U.S. followed, and another sixteen were rapidly added in the fifteen months after Trusthouse Forte took it over.

So, from 1935 to 1979, the group had grown by straight-forward expansion, acquisition and merger. A look at its results for 1978 gives the financial profile: a turnover of £613.8 million, trading profit of £70.1 million, profit after tax of £31.7 million and net cash resources at the end of the financial year of £56 million. How is this vast empire of 76,000 rooms and 3,000 food outlets governed? Sir Charles Forte, at the end of 1978, decided to step down from his position as Chief Executive (in which he worked a regular sixteen hour day) to the somewhat less arduous position (10 a.m. to 7 p.m. five days a week) of Executive Chairman. Eric Hartwell is now Vice Chairman and Chief Executive, (he was formerly joint Chief Executive with Sir Charles) Sir Leslie Joseph Vice Chairman and Rocco Forte, Sir Charles' only son among five daughters, is Deputy Chief Executive, as is Leonard Rosso who first joined Forte after the war

There are eleven other directors, and the Chairman of the Board is Lord Thorneycroft.

There has naturally been intense speculation in the press and elsewhere as to who is likely to succeed Sir Charles when

"Sir Charles with his son Rocco"

he retires. His father is on record as seeing Rocco Forte as "most probably" leading the company in due course provided he is "accepted and worthy of the job". Rocco, previously head of personnel and of Gardner Merchant Food Services (of which he remains Chairman), is 34. He read modern languages at Pembroke College, Oxford, later qualified as a chartered accountant and worked with his father as personal assistant. Although he has been accustomed to visit various parts of the Forte operation since his schooldays, and worked in his holidays in the kitchens of some of the London hotels and in the restaurant at London Airport, his most gruelling but useful period of training came when he took over at short notice the management of a hotel and restaurant in Cannes, which Trusthouse Forte was developing, because its manager became ill. Setting it up from scratch and getting it on its feet for a period of nine months was, as Rocco Forte has said, "the best possible experience I could have had" in helping him appreciate at first hand the pressures and problems that are faced by managers in the field.

Gardner Merchant Food Services Ltd. is the largest industrial caterer in Europe and serves 2,000 clients including schools, hospitals and various international companies with 200 million meals a year, expanding within the last few years into the Middle East and South Africa, and simultaneously developing its industrial cleaning services. It provides food for companies from boardroom to shop-floor, including a contract with Fords for 80,000 meals a day, and has recently entered into a partnership with Unilever in Belgium, Holland and Germany; Gardner Merchant provide the management. The company sees particularly good opportunities in West Germany, where industrial catering is not nearly so advanced as it is in Britain. The catering side of Trusthouse Forte, headed by its own Managing Director, Tito Chiandetti, accounts for about the same proportion of the group's turnover as the hotels do, but its profits are only around a third of those brought in by the latter, basically because of the much higher overheads in catering.

Popular catering is a strong branch of Trusthouse Forte and in the past few years one of the more successful has been the Little Chef chain comprising nearly 200 roadside grills aiming to provide a fairly hearty meal for about £2.50. The motorway service areas referred to earlier operate under the name Motor Chef and the associated petrol stations and shops are also under Trusthouse Forte management. On a busy day a motorway service station can be visited by as many as 40,000 people. Arrived at their destination, travellers are catered for by a hundred Quality Inns in towns and cities as well as Kardomah coffee houses. Further up-market are the twenty-eight Heneky Steak Bars and twelve first class restaurants, including Sir Charles' favourite Cafe Royal, the hunting Lodge and Gennaro's in the West End of London, and the George and Vulture in the City — another place with literary associations as it was well known to

Charles Dickens. The Royal Parks in London are a further preserve of the group, and the Serpentine Buffet in 1978 won a competition organised by the Department of the Environment.

Some twenty-five per cent of everything bought by Trusthouse Forte – and they spend nearly £300 million a year on supplies; including in 1978; 39 million pints of milk, 20 million eggs, 7.5 million loaves, 34,000 tons of meat and vegetables, 3 million glasses, 3 million pieces of crockery, 600,000 pieces of cutlery and 65 miles of carpet; from ashtrays and cutlery for hotels and restaurants to the food sold in them – goes through a centralised purchasing division, whose Director is Christopher Dams, a former director of purchasing in Europe for Avon Cosmetics. The group issues rigorous specifications to all its suppliers, but tries to avoid any supplier becoming too dependent on the group as his main outlet. Wine, tasted by a special management committee and approved before purchase, is all bought from Grierson Blumenthal, the London firm of wine merchants. There are central kitchens at Dunstable (a larger version of the pre-war centralised sandwich and bakery operation for the milk bars), and a group butchery in South London. The food depot system used for the hotels and restaurants within a sixty-mile radius of London has recently been extended by the acquisition of a chain of provincial distribution depots in Bournemouth, Rochdale, Leicester, Wotton-under-Edge and Cumbernauld. Fruit, vegetables and meat are transported in chilled trucks, and Trusthouse Forte prides itself that its specifications for food suppliers are considerably higher than the rest of the catering industry. Heavy emphasis is placed on quality control at branch level and through suppliers within and outside the group, and the technicians and biologists at their own Colnbrook Laboratory in West London carry out a continual programme of foodstuff analysis and collaborate with Trusthouse Forte chefs over new recipes. One part of the catering side constantly being extended is the group's 'own brand', Puritan Maid; products are made exclusively for Trusthouse Forte under this label, which enables close control of quality and of stock.

The hotels and restaurants within the company are not

absolutely obliged to buy food through the centralised purchasing operation, but any supplies they may wish to obtain locally have to be sanctioned and approved by it, however insignificant they may seem to be. Bulk orders for such items as cutlery are placed with manufacturers to cover a year's requirements at a time, and orders of bed linen, curtains and so on for use in hotels are planned on a system by which basic designs are chosen with several possible variants in colour and pattern, and the final choice is left to individual management.

One of the most highly organised aspects of the group's catering activities is that carried out for airlines and airports.

THF caters for 75 airlines from airports in Britain, France, Holland and Germany. Loading for an international flight.

Their Airport Services and its associated company, Airport Catering Services (the latter jointly owned with British

Airways) now provide in-flight meals for seventy-five airlines at twenty-four European airports. The group employs 1,500 catering staff in Europe, and as well as serving fifteen million meals a year, Airport Services clean and "dress" over nine thousand five hundred aircraft annually. They provide a full range of catering in the airports for passengers and staff, as well as a variety of shopping facilities such as duty free drink, tobacco and perfumes and other goods – not to mention such luxuries as fresh flowers in the first class. A phalanx of cleaners is employed on the turn-round operation, as well as large-scale waste-disposal which involves the rubbish being compressed and taken miles away for dumping. Much of the food is cooked in the company's own kitchens at the airports and elsewhere, and some idea of the complexity of this highly specialised business can be gained from the fact that a Boeing 747 setting off on a long-haul journey has to be loaded with approximately 10,000 separate items ranging from toothpicks to champagne buckets.

A natural extension of this has been an increasing involvement in travel services. Business, holiday and group travel are all covered, principal companies being W.F. and R.K. Swan, whose well-known Swan Tours offer archaeological and historical journeys in Europe accompanied by guest lecturers. Fourways Coach Tours and Milbanke Travel are other wholly owned subsidiaries; Trusthouse Forte had for some time an interest in Thomas Cook but sold this in 1970. Computerised hotel booking is now possible in more than eight hundred Trusthouse Forte hotels worldwide via an IBM computer system (the largest in the world of its kind) in Ealing, West London. It is available from 8.30 a.m. to 10 p.m. and employs forty staff working in shifts, each with a personal visual display unit which shows in seconds whether a reservation is possible; if the hotel is full, customers are immediately offered alternative accommodation at other company hotels in the same area. The computer system is linked to thirty Trusthouse Forte sales offices around the globe, some via satellite, and can produce all kinds of peripheral information, such as the distance from hotel to airport, and is currently making about 200,000 bookings a year.

The group is best known as hoteliers, and on those eight hundred-plus hotels its reputation ultimately rests. Trusthouse Forte occupancy rates in both Britain and France (where they own the George V, Plaza Athenee and La Tremoille in Paris) are higher than any other hotel group in either country. The hotels and restaurants are sharing a £25 million capital project for up-grading (£2 million was spent on the Waldorf a couple of years ago to restore it to its former Edwardian grandeur) in a programme designed to go on well into the 1980s, and Sir Charles would dearly like to build more as well as enlarging the group by acquisition. This ambition will be encouraged by the recent government grant of Industrial Building Allowances on new investment in hotel building after years of pressure from the hotel industry, though Trusthouse Forte would still like to see the initial allowance of twenty per cent increased to bring it into line with the fifty per cent enjoyed by other industries. Similarly the group views with disfavour the "iniquitous" Development Land Tax which it feels is in direct contradiction to the continual urging to encourage foreign visitors and take full advantage of foreign earnings generated by tourism. (Nearly half of Trusthouse Forte's guests in British hotels in 1978 came from overseas). The rating system could also certainly be reviewed, it feels, if London is to benefit from further new hotels; but Sir Charles is definitely not in favour of a government subsidy, feeling that it leads too easily to government control. The Post House programme, a group of hotels in the medium price bracket, was one sector of Trusthouse Forte hotel development which came to a halt some years ago, after thirty had been built, for these and various other reasons. It is now starting up again in a small way with a new one being built at Haydock, and feasibility studies for further building being carried out; Sir Charles has spoken recently of his ambition for an initial twenty, then another thirty, with perhaps a hundred altogether in the long term.

An application in 1978 to the now disbanded Price Commission by Trusthouse Forte for permission to raise their hotel tariffs in Britain was countered by a wide-ranging investigation by the Commission into the company's affairs and policies. Its result was gratifying, however, because in its report the Commission, while granting the requested rise, made an assessment that Trusthouse Forte "is a well-managed and forward looking company with a responsible attitude towards improving the efficiency of its operations and serving the consumer", and praising the standard of management, its staff relations, recruitment and training policies, sales promotion and control of costs and standards. Some of these aspects have been touched on already, and others will be described further on; meanwhile it is clear that international hotel management contracts are one of the growth areas in the group. It has established a new subsidiary company devoted exclusively to this, and under such a contract Trusthouse Forte becomes responsible for the operation and management of a hotel in return for a fee. Developments already secured under this scheme include new hotels in Bahrein, Dubai, Saudi Arabia, Tunisia and the U.S.A. Some of them are pretty spectacular by European standards; for instance the Plaza of the Americas in Dallas, Texas, is to cost $100 million. It will have 442 luxury bedrooms built round a central ice skating arena, with 25-storey office blocks on either side and incorporating an athletic club, tennis courts and a jogging track, as well as a convention centre. The Riyadh Palace will go some way to alleviate the acute shortage of hotel rooms in the administrative capital of Saudi Arabia, with 360 rooms designed principally for businessmen and within walking distance of most of the government ministries.

This management subsidiary company is run by John Lewis, who started his Trusthouse Forte career seventeen years ago as manager of the Cafe Royal and has since been in charge of hotels in the group in Britain and overseas. His company offers the enormous experience of Trusthouse Forte in all fields of hotel management, and equally important, marketing, which can be particularly valuable to would-be hoteliers in the developing countries. Although they do sometimes take over the management of existing hotels, the contracts are more often for new ones, where Trusthouse Forte is deeply involved from the earliest planning stages. The initial brief covers instructions to the architect

*Grosvenor House Hotel,
London*

*Hotel Plaza Athénée,
Paris*

Hyde Park Hotel, London

Bermudiana Hotel, Bermuda

Pierre Hotel, New York

Hotel George V, Paris

and essential building and construction specifications such as standards for elevators, sound-proofing and air conditioning as well as kitchens and other key areas, for which they act as general consultants. Once the hotel is built, if Trusthouse Forte is to act as managers it is usually for a period of at least twenty years, and this involves an overall marketing strategy which is drawn up about two years before the opening date and takes into account such factors as economic trends in the country concerned. The Al Jazira in Bahrain was the first of these ventures, which is now a going concern.

It is not generally appreciated that a hotel must be marketed in much the same way as any consumer product – with the added hazard that an empty hotel room is a 'wasted' asset, bearing nearly as many costs as an occupied one. (A figure usually adopted by the industry as a rule-of-thumb guide is for a break-even point of two-thirds full, so profit only begins above this level). Trusthouse Forte have been particularly skilful in their efforts to counteract the seasonal peaks and troughs of the hotel business. They have introduced for example, winter Bargain Breaks and special discounts for out of season and weekend visits, which many of their competitors have been quick to imitate. The hotels are marketed on the assumption that each, from the luxurious ones of the European capitals to the smallest Post House or motel in the group, has its own individual character and atmosphere; an effort is made to see that it fits in with its locality or region, and each is responsible for building up its own business in its own local market; likewise each manager is responsible for his own profitability. The group itself offers an overall marketing strategy aimed at creating hotel business generally and stepping up demand where needed. One example is the build-up of conference centres; in Britain alone, Trusthouse Forte operate over a thousand different venues for conferences, the largest of which can take two thousand people.

A team of 300 sales staff operate throughout the world, 74 of them in the U.S., and it is backed up by a large volume of market research, discovering what clients want from their hotels and looking at countries of origin. (Some of the most effective market research is often the simplest – when the group was considering buying the Waldorf, Eric Hartwell went to stay in it, and later did the same thing in the George V in Paris, while two fellow directors stayed in La Tremoille and Plaza Athenee when these three hotels were being evaluated). Currently they are aiming at increasing the volume of sales from West Germany and other Continental countries and America. The success of their strategies is underlined by the fact that, as mentioned before, the group's occupancy rate is better than average for the industry, particularly in the off-season when it is nearly fifteen per cent more than the national figure. In keeping with the overall Trusthouse Forte philosophies of cost effectiveness, the marketing, advertising and sales efforts are scrutinised in each country on the basis of what expenditure is necessary in order to produce a given number of visitors.

Sir Charles speaks in terms of 'trimming' the development of the group to a certain range of undertakings which are relevant to one another — "I don't want to buy aeroplanes or ships" — and avoiding the imbalances of a conglomerate. The leisure side of the business is still small, but forms an integral part of the package that Trusthouse Forte can offer the traveller and/or holidaymaker. The initial investment in The Talk Of The Town has been followed by a similar venture in Birmingham, the Night Out theatre-restaurant; they own three piers with all the attendant amusement arcades, bars and cafes — one is the North Pier, one of Blackpool's most famous landmarks; a number of theatres and concert halls, dolphinaria and three holiday villages including one in Sardinia, the Forte Village Club (run on Club Mediterranee lines) and one nearer home, in St. Ives, Cornwall. All these come under the supervision of THF Leisure Ltd. set up in 1970. Retail interests are principally geared to airport shopping, but Lillywhites of Piccadilly Circus is a recent acquisition, selling sports equipment and clothing there and at branches in Edinburgh, Leeds and Croydon. Lillywhites is also concerned with the design and equipment of sports stadia and multi-sport centres in the U.K. and overseas, as well as manufacturing, under the brand name Cantabrian, athletics equipment which has been regularly used at the Olympic Games since the end of the last war.

While Trusthouse Forte is indisputably a huge multinational corporation, it sees future growth and development springing from the twin foundations of the U.S.A. and the U.K. In only five years the American operation has grown to the point where it contributes £11 million to group profits, and Trusthouse Forte Inc., the North American subsidiary, is responsible for nearly two-thirds of the entire complement of THF hotels. The TraveLodge operation, masterminded from San Diego by an Australian, Roger Manfred, President and Chief Executive Officer of THF Inc., is the keystone of future U.S. expansion, and presents a glowing example, having been 'turned round' and tripled its profits in the quarter ending 31st January 1979. Sir Charles, who has paid frequent and generous tribute to Manfred's judgement and managerial capacity, makes no secret of his ambition to see the U.S. operation equal in size to the British end of the company, and the money for such an expansion is readily available for a group which as the American press has reverently noted, "makes more money even than Holiday Inns".

As well as participation via development and management schemes, THF Inc. is all set to build new hotels in a number of principal cities throughout the States, from New York, Washington and Philadelphia to San Francisco and Los Angeles – with the idea that, like the Westbury Hotels in Manhattan and the West End of London, they should rank among the handful of the very best hotels in each city. The cost of such undertakings is breathtaking to anybody without the financial strengths of a Sir Charles Forte, being unlikely to fall short of £18 to £20 million apiece. Here again they are likely to be developed in partnership schemes, with limited liability, financed by mortgage arrangements with some of the 'top ten' life assurance companies in the States. Each hotel, of around 400 rooms will be created with strongly individual characters, just like their smaller brethren in Europe. Convention business – a fast growth area in almost all the developed countries in the world – is another area in to which Trusthouse Forte intends to expand in North America, and Manfred forecasts "at least ten" major convention centres, each capable of accommodating between 1,000 and 5,000 people, in operation over the next eight years.

Like the new hotels, they will be built in major cities and under similar partnership schemes, but they will be strongly 'brand-oriented', with the big guns of Trusthouse Forte's management expertise directed at the vast and as yet far from fully tapped potential market of 200 million people.

As well as hotel know-how, in all areas from choice of site to purchase of coffee cups (and a sales and marketing strength which has dovetailed neatly with the TraveLodge activity), Trusthouse Forte has taken across the Atlantic a relatively unfamiliar emphasis on food as a major source of profit and growth. Food and beverage are apt to be discountted as profit earners by U.S. hoteliers, but for Trusthouse Forte they already account for forty per cent of their U.S. turnover and are expected to reach fifty per cent. The profits of Colony Kitchen, the chain of medium priced restaurants in California, have rocketed since the acquisition. Like those of TraveLodge, they were earning about £400,000 per year when Trusthouse Forte bought them, but this has subsequently shot up to over a million pounds in one quarter alone.

Some of the aspects of expansion in Britain and Europe have been touched on already — the continuing upgrading and modernisation of hotels as well as capital investment in new ones. The Little Chef and Henekys operations in particular, and City Centre, are earmarked for extension over the next five years or so, but some novel plans are to be tried out in motorway service stations. (A recent government investigation was held into these which, while recognising the difficulties they face, with staff working under great pressure and often in isolated places, paid tribute to the staff loyalty and team spirit which exists in them. It also acknowledged that the terms of operation, fixed by the government, impose rigid restrictions on management). It is in these potentially difficult cafeterias that THF Catering are injecting their new idea for the eighties; fast food on quasi-American lines but with more style and elegance. If they succeed there, the scheme will be adapted to City Centre operations where it should be easier to put into effect — another instance of the corporate insistence on what Catering Director Chiandetti has described as "changing the catering formula to meet the requirements of the times".

So . . . a multimillion, multinational company with seventy-two thousand employees springing from a milk bar established in London less than fifty years ago. What are the tenets of the philosophy behind such growth? To Sir Charles Forte the

Signing the distinguished visitors book in the City Chambers, Glasgow, 1979; with the Lord Provost of Glasgow, David Hodge.

question has a simple answer. "There are two basic principles to life as an entrepreneur: (a) Hard work. (b) Believe in people and have trust. When I started at the age of twenty-six with a milk bar in Regent Street, there were just a few people; I had to earn their respect, treat them properly, work with them, set them an example. The same principles apply now. Then, I ran it myself, saw that things got done. Now, with a turnover approaching £700 million and seventy-two thousand employees, the philosophy, principles and basic thought remain the same — I achieve the same things through other people".

In other words, delegation to trusted lieutenants — some,

but not all of whom have been mentioned in this study of Trusthouse Forte – who can and will ensure the continuation of the company along the lines laid down by Sir Charles.

The company philosophy has been formulated in a seven point statement as follows:

1. *To increase profitability and earnings per share each year in order to encourage investment and to improve and expand the business.*
2. *To give complete customer satisfaction by efficient and courteous service, with value for money.*
3. *To support managers and their staff in using personal initiative to improve the profit and quality of their operations, whilst observing the company's policies.*
4. *To provide good working conditions and to maintain effective communications at all levels to develop better understanding and assist decision making.*
5. *To ensure no discrimination against sex, race, colour or creed and to train, develop and encourage promotion within the company based on merit and ability.*
6. *To act with integrity at all times and to maintain a proper sense of responsibility towards the public.*
7. *To recognise the importance of each and every employee who contributes towards these aims.*

Training, Sir Charles emphasises, cannot be over estimated. "It is an essential part of any skill and especially in this industry where so many skills are required. It goes on all the time, you learn something every day – certainly a youngster in a hotel or restaurant should be learning every day". There is an extensive training programme, probably one of the finest in the industry, within the Trusthouse Forte group, and a good £3 million a year is spent on it. In 1978, for example, the group took on about 2,700 young people, 1,000 of them straight from school and university, who joined a variety of apprenticeships and management training schemes; and this was during a period of high national unemployment, especially among school leavers.

As well as the hundred and fifty training specialists at centres such as the Gardner Merchant training school at

Eastbourne, who teach every element of hotel management and catering, there are more than 4,000 'on the job' trainers working in the field. Senior management is also involved in training – it is the company's firm belief that it represents an investment not only in helping staff to make their best possible contribution to success as a group, but also because it encourages them to realise their full potential and thus increases their job satisfaction. Sir Charles has recently and intriguingly hinted at the possible inception of an 'in-house' THF University of Catering and Hotel Keeping, which would start with courses in management and then broaden its scope to take in marketing and selling, and public relations, "because every type of experience and expertise, from architects to research chemists and financial experts, are required in a business like ours". It is one of the advantages of size, he adds, that the bigger the group becomes, "the more it can afford to do those things which would be impossible if it were medium sized or small."

The recognition of the importance of every employee, with however humble a role in the company's affairs, has always been an article of faith with Sir Charles from his earliest days as an employer, and he recognises that one of the main reasons for the success of his company is that first he and now Trusthouse Forte, have always paid better wages than the industry in general, and looks after staff better. It is also one of the prime reasons for the lack of unionisation in the group – "something of a phenomenon" as he puts it.

The protection of the freedom of the individual is an important part of the philosophy of Sir Charles and his company, and is linked with his strongly and frequently voiced dislike of bullies – "I won't have any bullying of any kind in any way. And *I* won't be bullied – I won't have anyone telling *me* what to do and how to run my business". In fact barely ten per cent of THF employees have joined a union, and those are mostly in transport and "never quibble over the hours of work necessary". There has only been one strike since the company was formed, it had a lot of publicity, but was not supported by the majority of staff in the establishments concerned and was speedily and satisfactorily settled. (Terry's, the chocolate company, was highly unionised but did not remain long within the group, and when there was a hint of union trouble at The Talk Of The Town Sir Charles was widely reported as being ready to sell rather than give in, though in the event this proved unnecessary).

Wages can be as much as fifty per cent higher than for comparable jobs elsewhere, and staff turnover – in an industry which too often complacently accepts sky-high turnover rates with their consequent waste of time and training – is falling every year. Managers and executives rarely leave, and this again Sir Charles attributes to the group emphasis on training, as each employee, regardless of rank, is taught to do a good job himself and to see that those for whom he is responsible are happy and content. Staff consultative committee meetings are an important feature of THF company life, (hotel and restaurant managers are required to chair them) and staff are to some extent trained to be "welfare officers as well as managers" as Sir Charles puts it.

He does not dismiss outside management training from say, Harvard, Manchester or other business schools, but is emphatic that some practical experience is necessary first – "get in some business background and experience, then some business school, then business again". It's difficult to adjust, he argues, if all a person has had is academic training; when he gets in among the practical difficulties he finds everything is not just 'laid down the line' as in text book situations.

The father of six children comes to the surface when he likens dealing with subordinates to family life; "You can be, you must be, stern, strict or demanding – it doesn't matter as long as you are fair. Just as with your family you have to be strict but loving, so in business you must be strict but fair. You should expect people to do their job and do their duty, not mollycoddle them"; but he concedes that this can be a problem in business today "because it's not always expected in management or along the line".

When you have to impose your will in business, he believes most firmly that you should do so without damage. "I'd rather lose a bit of business than damage someone

SIR CHARLES FORTE
International Host

Welcoming former President Richard Nixon to the Hyde Park Hotel.

With Lynden Pindling, Prime Minister of the Bahamas.

Sir Charles with the Rt Hon. James Prior M.P. and Lord Delfont.

A specially bound edition of the Gideon Bible presented to Sir Charles in 1978 by The Gideon International president in Britain. There is a Gideon Bible in every THF hotel bedroom.

through my fault", he avers; and this is particularly applicable when the group is selling something: "We tell them what we are selling, let them have a jolly good look, point out the snags. They can't turn round then and say Forte sold us this, but it wasn't worth the price! We tell them what the price is, and say when you've thought about it, let us know." However, THF is more likely to be buying than selling, and it owes its enormously successful record of growth to skilful acquisitions. Asked what he looks for in new purchases, Sir Charles first replies by quoting the late Conrad Hilton's dictum that there were three things important in buying a hotel — site, site and site. "But I would change that to site, site and management". If a well-sited hotel enjoys really good management, the whole thing becomes so much easier.

Just as he sized up the site and potential of his first milk bars, so the group now attempts by feasibility studies to estimate turnover and profit of any proposed new hotel or restaurant, or chain of them, aiming at between twenty and thirty per cent on the money invested, bearing in mind the cost of money reflected in today's high interest rates. The company "borrows continually", usually owing between £2 and £3 hundred million at any time and paying interest of around £17 million a year, "but the proportion of loans to assets is what matters" as Sir Charles points out. "New hotels must conform to our standards — or be capable of improvement". Sometimes a hotel that is badly run by another company offers a better chance of being turned round to make a profit. But there are times, he says, when the efforts of highly skilled personnel are wasted and it can be for a variety of reasons, of which bad site is usually one, and the company could never make a success of it. "If we can't, then we must sell, even at a loss — but it's quite possible that a personal owner might be able to make a go of it, live on the spot and carry it off."

The genuine enthusiasm felt by Sir Charles for all aspects of living in and managing a hotel or restaurant (although he is under no illusions about the disadvantages of inordinately long and 'unsocial' hours) shines through any conversation with him. "There's a lot of satisfaction to be had in running a hotel. It's splendid, because you — and your wife — are there, it's a true pleasure to see it running perfectly. A good existence". But he adds — "it's not *my* way of life. I've always been ambitious, and I still have ambitions. There are things I still want to do, make more profit, make things better".

One significant strong point of the Trusthouse Forte group, recognised by the rest of the industry, is that the hotel managers enjoy the freedom to run their hotels almost as subsidiary companies and have complete control over all aspects of their hotel operations. Obviously they must work within the framework of the group's philosophies and capital expenditure programmes, but within these limitations they have the freedom to 'get on with the job', calling on help and advice from the central organisation if they need it. This was noted by the Price Commission when it commented: "Great emphasis is placed on the responsibility of line management. It is our view that a good balance has been achieved between local autonomy and central direction, which must be conducive to efficiency."

One area of 'central direction' which Sir Charles particularly relishes is the examination of the individual balance sheets of the 'units' that go to make up his mighty empire. "I really enjoy balance sheets — and figures can be romantic, you know, and tell a story quite clearly. I can look at a list of figures and see that the turnover is good, the hotel's doing well, the price is right — or perhaps this manager here is not doing so well, he is not a good controller; let's see how we can help him; the figures are dropping, turnover's down — perhaps the hotel needs re-decorating?"

As well as reading the figures, Sir Charles tirelessly visits all the units, "looking and seeing", as he puts it, though he doesn't make a habit of dropping in unannounced, feeling that "if they can't do it when they know I'm coming, then they can't do it at all". He likes talking, discussing, being in the middle of the business, and, a devoted father and grandfather himself, he makes a point of asking about the wives and families of his employees and is genuinely interested in their replies.

Now more than ever, as THF has such a great commitment

31

in the United States, he has to travel a good deal, which he tends to do in blocks of six weeks or a month at a time, looking not only at the group's current possessions and interests, but as always, with a sharp eye open for possible acquisitions or development opportunities. He is well aware of the stress and fatigue of business travel, and tries to persuade his own executives when they go abroad, particularly on long flights, to go a day or two early, or stay on for a weekend after the business is done – though he rarely takes his own advice, and in practice hardly any of them can ever spare the time. But "relaxation is very necessary" he feels, "the mind must have rest too, as well as the body", and he loves fishing, shooting and golf, as well as sailing his yacht in the Mediterranean.

What other precepts has Sir Charles followed in the course of such an illustrious business career? "I'm awfully cautious. I'm not a wheeler-dealer and I always make sure, never take too long a step. Although I don't really enjoy negotiations, because I'm too anxious to see the end product, I like deals occasionally when I know that they have been well thought out, but I never move on my own. I take advice, I listen to the opinion of professionals, bankers, solicitors, before I do anything. I've been lucky, but I've been foreseeing – though I have made a few mistakes. Events have caught up with me once or twice in my personal life and I've had difficulties with money, but always my *personal* money, not the company's. We as a company are trustees for other people's money and we must be continually aware of that. A lot of pension funds, for example, may be really dependent on us, relying on us for money for people in sickness and old age, and I think we must be as concerned about that kind of investment as the large institutions, or maybe more so. I also think one must have a personal stake in the business; if one is at the head of it – it makes one turn out the lights when one leaves the room!" he adds with a twinkle.

Punctuality, accessibility and consistency are other cornerstones of the Forte philosophy. Extremely punctual himself ("though I'm not as punctual as Eric Hartwell", he concedes ruefully – "if he says he'll ring at 3.30 it's 3.30 *on the dot*") he expects others to be so too, and if he spots someone

Sailing, along with golf and fishing are among Sir Charles' favourite outdoor interests.

waiting to see a manager he is quite likely to ask how long they have been there, then telephone the manager himself to tell him his visitor has already been waiting for ten minutes. "It's an absolute cardinal sin in this company, unpunctuality". Similarly, he practises his own precepts by being accessible to his colleagues. His office door is rarely shut, his personal secretaries, he says, know his private affairs, and his colleagues know they can always get hold of him when necessary. "And I do the same things every day, so that people know what to expect. I always do my correspondence — it's polite to reply as soon as possible — I value consistency and I think inconsistency is equivalent to selfishness".

The hotel and catering industry is of enormous and growing importance to the British economy — it employs directly over 2 million people (almost eight per cent of the country's workforce) and indirectly gives employment to many thousands of others through its huge demand for supplies. Sir Charles points out that in spite of Trusthouse Forte's vast size, the group represents only a small part of British industry, although it makes a significant contribution to the domestic economy. Even more important, it helps the U.K. balance of payments, in spite of inflation which hits the catering industry particularly hard as so much of its raw material — food — must be imported.

Pondering on the economic problems of Britain, with inflation, high tax rates and rates of interest, Sir Charles agrees that to start today hoping to achieve what he did "would certainly be more difficult, but there's no doubt that young people just beginning their careers, who are entrepreneurially minded, *can* make a success". If more people would be prepared to work hard "contribute a penny and a bit of effort", he is convinced that Britain could once more be a world power.

TERENCE CONRAN
International Designer

If you look up 'habitat' in the dictionary, you will find it
means the locality in which an animal or plant naturally lives
– but hundreds of thousands of people in Europe have no
need to do this simple research. They know quite well what
the word means, and they spell it with a capital H. It is a
chain of shops owned and run by Terence Conran, undoubtedly one of the most influential British designers of the
twentieth century, and now the Chairman of the £50 million
Habitat Design Holdings Ltd. of which his forty-six shops
(including those in America known as Conran's), form
the retail showcase for some of the output of Conran and his
design team. To anyone who has ever shopped in them, or
just looked in the windows or the Habitat catalogue, the
word conveys a strong but simple image – natural pine,
ceramic tiles, furniture in clear colours and unfussy shapes,
pottery and glass of the cleanest and purest lines, these are a
few of the elements going to make up the total Habitat 'look'.

Conran, who was born in 1931, loved drawing and making
things even as a child. At school at Bryanston he took metal-
work and engineering, and learnt pottery from an inspired
teacher, called Don Potter, who taught him how to make and
fire earthenware and slipware; he later built his own wood-
fired kiln (sometimes staying up all night to keep it burning)
and sold some of his handiwork to friends and relations.
He also made models, some on an ambitious scale such as a

three foot replica of H.M.S. Hood, some rather more unusual, including tiny interiors fitted inside matchboxes. "I actually wanted to be a gunsmith when I left school", Conran recalls, "not that I particularly liked shooting but I loved making things and was attracted to sporting guns". He dropped this idea when he discovered it involved a ten-year apprenticeship. Another school interest had been organic chemistry and he had carried out some work on the properties of dyestuffs; someone suggested he combine this with his outstanding drawing ability to become a textile designer. "I hardly knew what a textile designer was at that stage, but the suggestion seemed like a stroke of genius". He took his portfolio and his work on dyes to the Central School of Arts and Crafts, (now the Central School of Art and Design) and "to my own amazement and that of everyone else, I got in, and started to learn what design was all about. But although I was, and still am, fascinated by textiles, I soon felt I needed to widen my interests, and after eighteen months I left and got a job". He worked at £8 a week for the Rayon Industry, which, enormously profitable at the end of the war, had lavish premises in Upper Grosvenor Street, which they ran as an exhibition centre, decorated by Dennis Lennon with an extravagance and panache which was particularly conspicuous in those austerity years. Conran worked on a magazine put out by the Rayon Industry and stayed there happily for a year, until it became obvious that his employers' funds were not as sizeable as they had thought. Lennon offered him a job, at the same salary, in his own private interior design practice which Conran accepted.

By this time he had a growing interest in designing furniture, and shared a studio with the sculptor Eduardo Paolozzi; "I taught him to weld, he taught me about the aesthetic appreciation of three-dimensional objects". Conran began to make furniture for his own use and pleasure, with no idea of selling it. With Lennon, he worked on the interior of a hotel in Lusaka and also on the design of a quantity of furniture for the Festival of Britain. "There was very little modern furniture around at this time. We made some for the Scottish Manufacturers' Association, and we designed textiles for a company called David Whitehead, run by a Dr. Murray".

One of Conran's fabric designs for ticking was then accepted by Myers the bedding firm and sold a million yards which seemed incredible to him. He was also asked as a freelance to carry out a study for a Manchester firm making up denims into work clothes and boiler suits, to see if there were any other possible uses for the material. A suggestion that it could become fashionable for leisure wear was, however, greeted with some scorn by the company, who failed to act on it.

The Festival of Britain ended without any evidence of the renascence of British industry nor of British design which had been fervently expected of it; Lennon's firm had virtually no work and Conran found himself out of a job. After a period of freelance work for Edinburgh Weavers, he was employed by Simpsons to do their window display where he worked with Natasha Kroll, now famous for her stage and TV sets, and they collaborated on a book on display. Some of his experiences when working in the distinctive convex windows on Simpson's Piccadilly facade were quite bizarre; starting at 6 p.m. at night, the designers were the focus of some curiosity from passers-by, and Conran recalls one occasion when, to add further realism to a display of executive suits, he was bending over a blotter on an office desk and attempting to write a facsimile of a signature that had just been blotted, when glancing up, he received a sympathetic nod from an elderly woman tramp on the pavement outside — "she recognised that I was as dotty as she was".

As well as dressing their windows, Conran was now making some furniture for Simpsons which they used in the store, and one August they offered him an exhibition in the shoe department, to liven it up a bit at a period when sales are usually slack. He was given an area of ten square feet in which he showed a selection of his work, "tables, shelves, chairs, all modern and brightly coloured, and some planters and huge terracotta pots I had made". There was virtually nothing of this sort available commercially in Britain at that time. The big manufacturers, such as Lebus and Beautility were producing ranges of conventional pieces like over-stuffed three-piece suites, and the designers who influenced

Conran's developing style were all from overseas, "Charles Eames, George Nelson, and a few from Italy — we used to go to the Triennale Exhibition like moths to a lamp".

After his exhibition in Simpsons, things slowly started to happen. He began receiving orders, often working until 3 a.m. to finish an intricate piece of welding, and now moved into a house recently vacated by a company of A.T.S., with a large basement flat he could use as a workshop, at a very low rent. Materials were still desperately scarce, particularly metal, and he relied heavily on friendly foremen of building sites selling off various items such as reinforcing rods, and also managed to track down a fabric supplier in Bethnal Green. Transport too, was difficult, and delivering bulky pieces of completed furniture to his customers by means of the London underground was an unforgettable experience. This did however give birth to his idea of delivering furniture in sections in a flat construction package; the 'KD' or knock-down system which has proved so successful in the Habitat shops and been widely taken up by other manufacturers.

Among his customers at this time was Ian McCullum, editor of the *Architectural Review*, who commissioned Conran to make furniture for both his office and his own apartment, and, by a rather devious route, the John Lewis Partnership. Although the furniture buyers would not order Conran's furniture, an "amazing lady" on the sales staff, deeply interested in furniture design and manufacture, infiltrated some of his pieces into her department by an ingenious scheme by which she ordered them a few at a time as special orders for customers — always the same ones, a "Mr. and Mrs. Stock". Mr. and Mrs. Stock then cancelled their order, leaving the redoubtable Mrs. Horne triumphantly in possession, to re-sell to the more discriminating customers of John Lewis.

Up until now, in 1953, Conran had handled everything himself, with no employees, but it was becoming apparent that he would have to take on new, larger premises and some extra people to help him if he was to continue. He rented a workshop under the Ballet Rambert in Notting Hill Gate, "not many tenants wanted a ballet company thumping

about overhead", and yet another basement, a small showroom in Piccadilly Arcade under a flower shop for what now
seems the incredibly low rent of thirty shillings (£1.50) a
week. "I started to employ people, usually fairly unqualified,
to do some of the welding". He also made himself into a
limited company, taking the name Conran and Co., ready
formed from a company his father had started before the war
importing gum copal. After the war the business had been
badly hit by the introduction of synthetic resins, and when
a fire gutted the East End factory the company became
moribund and his father joined a paint firm. He therefore
presented Conran and Co. to his son (which also had some
useful accumulated tax losses) to form the nucleus of the
future business structure.

"Now the business began to take off". Conran and Co.
produced a catalogue which was circulated to architects,
who formed the bulk of its customers and specified Conran
furniture for use in new offices, hospitals, hotels and restaurants. "But our finances were still on a very hand to mouth
basis — I had to get the money for a commission on delivery
of the furniture, or I couldn't buy the materials for the
next batch, and a late payment could cause havoc. I had a
few hundreds from my family, but I needed a larger sum —
about £1,000 or so — to buy proper workshop machinery".
He discussed his predicament with Ian Storey, a psychia-
trist who had been with the Army in Korea and owned the
house in Kensington where Conran had a flat. Storey also
needed money, and together they decided the quickest way
to make some might be to start up some restaurants or
cafes. Storey thought of buying up an existing cafe, but
Conran, who always loved good food, wanted to start an
entirely new concept. "I visualised something extremely
simple, a small menu based on soup — we could make all
sorts of different soups from a basic stock without the
need of chefs — French bread, Cheddar cheese and espresso
coffee", then all the rage in London. They drove to Milan
and bought a second-hand Gaggia coffee machine and found
a woman who made "marvellous apple flans". Thinking
they ought first to know something about the restaurant
business, Conran with typical attention to basic principles

"The original soup kitchen, 1956"

went to Paris and worked for a couple of months in the two star Mediterranee restaurant near the Odeon, as washer-up and vegetable boy, "*Extremely* hard work, and it taught me a lot about producing high quality food, and about life in general, I returned to London a wiser person".

Storey and Conran opened their first Soup Kitchen, a name apt to bring a warm glow of nostalgia to those who were young in London in the early and mid 1950s. "It was very simple, with pine boarded walls — quite new at that time — quarry tiled floor, tile-topped tables and cane seated chairs I had made in the workshop", recalls Conran of their first venture in Chandos Place. "And we had a marvellous stroke of luck. On the day we opened we had invited the press, the Evening News and the Standard, when who should pour in but about forty-two tramps from the Covent Garden area, who had seen the name Soup Kitchen and turned up for a free meal". They were each given a bowl of soup, but told they would have to pay 1/6d for it another time, and the whole episode made an excellent news story. The high quality of the food, and its relative cheapness, confirmed the initial success and the partners went on to open a chain of Soup Kitchens, including one in Shoe Lane, just off Fleet Street, where they had the bright but short-lived idea of installing plug-in telephones for reporters to 'phone in their stories. The only failure was in Cambridge; the large premises were always packed with three hundred under-graduates, and everyone thought it must be making a fortune, but each student bought only one cup of coffee and settled in for the evening, so takings were "almost nil".

Soon Storey wanted to enlarge the scope of the restaurants and have a more elaborate menu which would have involved chefs, but for Conran the charm of the operation lay in its simplicity, and his partner therefore bought him out for £2,500 — "just what I needed to carry on".

Using this capital as a basis, Conran and Co. expanded rapidly during the rest of the 1950s. Conran took new workshop premises, first in Don Place in Chelsea and then in an old disused horse-bus garage in the North End Road. He needed still more room, and therefore bought another horse-bus garage in Camberwell, making over a derelict property to house a newly formed textile company involved in 'converting', i.e. buying the cloth and having it printed. They increased their sales through architects and began to design and build exhibition stands and carry out simple shop fitting. By 1960, Conran was employing around one hundred and twenty people in his two factories and in the offices and design side. "But financially it was still not on a really sound footing. We made some money one year, lost some the next – but somehow we managed to inch forward. There was a lot of new building in the late 1950s and we were one of the very few concerns making suitable furniture. By then we were producing quite a sophisticated range in metal and wood, and began to do upholstery".

The company now had a stroke of luck arising out of the considerable increase in property values. The local council wanted Conran's North End Road site for housing, and London Transport needed his Camberwell premises in connection with extension of the underground system. In addition, Conran had just learnt of the current LCC 'expanded town' scheme, intended to move some of the overspill population from central London into New Towns. He was taken on a tour of possible sites and picked out one in Thetford, Norfolk, as "just right". A 40,000 square foot factory would be built to his own specifications and leased to his company. Meanwhile it was the company's job to do what Conran describes as "one of the most fascinating things I have ever been involved in – persuading our workforce, or about one hundred people from it, to move to Thetford. Taking them there, showing them houses, schools, the countryside, letting them get the feel of the place, arranging for them to see local newspapers and so on. They weren't in the least pushed into it, but they had to let us know by a certain date whether they would come or not. Then we had to train up local people so they would be able to start work when the factory opened. It was like a re-birth, to have a proper modern factory with new equipment like a timber mill – everything we had previously bought had been second-hand – to move from wretched, rubbishy, down-at-heel surroundings to something that was absolutely new".

It was not an easy period even when the move had been

been accomplished. His employees were used to 'workshop techniques' rather than the more sophisticated and organised system which the expanded business now required of them, and further difficulties ensued as the result of a general downturn in the economy. To counteract this, Conran decided the time had come to launch a proper range of domestic furniture; he made up some prototypes, showed them at the Furniture Exhibition at Earl's Court, and started production. They sold "reasonably well" from the start. The John Lewis Partnership (now on a more regular basis than the original 'Mr. and Mrs. Stock' system) being an important and helpful client in several ways. They paid promptly, within seven days of delivery, and were also one of the few retailers who agreed to take the furniture in the 'KD' state, others insisting on it being delivered assembled so they could inspect it.

Conran continued to make a certain amount of money on property deals, which helped to finance the output of the Thetford factory. Various offices in obscure buildings

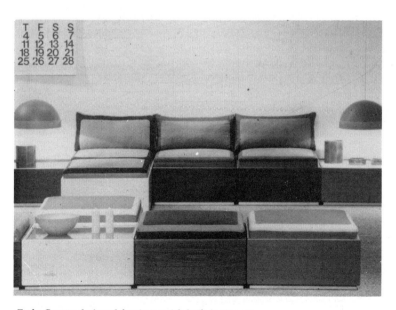

Early Conran-designed furniture with built-in storage.

45

of which he bought leases very cheaply — one was an old Jewish school behind St. Giles' Circus — quickly appreciated in value as office space became harder to come by and property values generally began to rise. By the spring of 1963 the Conran range of domestic furniture was selling in about two hundred furniture shops in the U.K.; the Scots, always interested in and receptive to new design, being particularly good customers, and today the Scottish Habitat stores are among the most successful. Conran and his sales manager decided to tour round the country and visit a cross section of the shops selling his furniture, in order to see for themselves exactly how it was being displayed and handled. They returned deeply depressed.

We realised there was no real chance of it succeeding, says Conran. "We had travelled round the country to about thirty or forty stores and not one was displaying it effectively — it was higgledy-piggledy with a few bits of modern furniture, some Scandinavian pieces, some fireside chairs, a lot of reproduction furniture and some G Plan, all crowded together. We also noticed the stores were practically empty except on Saturday mornings, had no style, trying to offer something for everybody who came into the store and were often scruffy. We knew we would continue to get a trickle of orders, but would never do any big business that way". They pondered the possibilities of "a better sort of furniture shop".

Encouraged by the current success of Mary Quant who for similar reasons — the inability or unwillingness of retailers to display her strikingly up-to-the-minute clothes in any correspondingly imaginative way — had recently opened a shop in Knightsbridge, designed by Conran, and was experiencing rocketing sales. The only shops, Conran felt, which gave a better than average attention to display were Heals (pretty expensive) and John Lewis, but there was no shop at all entirely dedicated to selling reasonably priced, modern furniture to young people. Martin Moss, the youthful manager of Woollands, was extremely interested but Woollands formed part of the Debenham Group and his hands were partly tied by group policy, and the necessity of selling "millinery to elderly ladies" under the same roof as the elegant furniture department. "So we thought, we'll open a shop ourselves, and we'll show 'em".

Conran and his colleagues devoted much thought to their prospective shop, and one of their first (and as it turned out, crucial) decisions was that it should not sell just furniture, giving rise to the empty, echoing spaces they had noticed on their tour – an emptiness which was decidedly putting off for any customers who might be around, and also tended to make the staff bored and discontented. "We wanted above all a busy, cheerful and active ambience for the furniture", emphasises Conran, "and we decided to sell all the other things that go with it. Glass, china, kitchen things – at a time when, thanks largely to Elizabeth David's cookery books, there was a resurgence of interest in cooking – textiles, our own and other people's, lighting, floor coverings, everything in fact which blended with the style of our own furniture".

They took great pains – and had a great deal of fun – choosing the merchandise, and recruited a lot of enthusiastic and interested young people to work in the new shop, which was opened in 1964 opposite the splendid tiled Michelin building at the top of Fulham Road. The name Habitat was chosen by combing through Roget's Thesaurus, and has been a singularly happy choice because it can be used with similar effect throughout Europe. The company has registered the name as far as possible in all the countries in the world where they feel it likely they may wish to open in the future, although it is not possible to retain exclusive use of it unless and until they start trading in the country concerned. The shop was a success from the first. It had an enormous amount of publicity, nearly all favourable, and Conran particularly remembers a glowing article in the Sunday Times. Helped by the presence of various small Italian restaurants in the area it rapidly became a favourite meeting place for young people – fashionable and relaxed - and they bought. "Turnover wasn't wildly exciting but it certainly was profitable. Other retailers thought we were just part of the "swinging Chelsea" scene, and said 'it's all right there, but you'll never make a go of it in Manchester. We were worried too, as we thought the established retailers might refuse to deal with a manufacturer who was now also a retailer". These fears proved groundless, and Conran recognises how lucky he has been that the rest of the retail did not wake up until the last few years to Habitat's great success, and therefore there was little competition while they were still establishing themselves.

"We got enormous pleasure from retailing" Conran recalls now. "We were in immediate contact with our own customers for the first time, saw their reaction on the spot to a new item and could find out what they really wanted to buy. And

Habitat, Fulham Road, London. Opened 1964. Became Conran Shop 1973.

we fairly revelled in all the publicity!" Seeing how often parents brought small children shopping with them, for example, gave Conran the idea of adding a range of toys to the items on sale. In spite of the success of this first shop however, the established furniture and department stores continued to sell his furniture in the same uninspired way. "So, very cautiously, we decided to become a chain, and within two years we had opened another shop in Tottenham Court Road, and then one in Manchester. By 1968 we had five shops. We started to become genuinely profitable, and to be more professional. We instituted a proper form of stock control and brought in management from outside, forming a sound management team".

Not every shop, of course, was entirely successful. Conran emphasizes the important part property plays in a retail operation − a wrong decision can be disastrous, while the right property or site can make large sums. The two major errors Habitat made in opening new shops have both been mistakes in the choice of situation. One was in Bolton, where in spite of what appeared to be a good catchment area, they never generated enough turnover to make the operation worthwhile, but a good property deal took much of the sting out of closing it down, as they were able to sell the premises at a profit. The other unsuccessful store, which came later, was in France at Les Ullis. A Habitat shop was opened in a large shopping mall outside Paris, next to a Carrefour hypermarket. "We thought the middle class, who are our basic customers everywhere, would come to the hypermarket to buy their food and would also then buy our products. But the Carrefour customers were much more down-market, and they came, loaded their 'chariots', the French word for trolleys, with about £40 worth of goods and went straight home".

As the U.K. chain slowly built up, Conran still felt bedevilled, as he had from the start, by lack of sufficient capital to put into operation all the "marvellous ideas" that were constantly coming to him and his enthusiastic young colleagues. It was a constant source of frustration, and when in 1967 he was approached by the Reed Paper Group with an idea for a joint venture, the Conran team were greatly excited. Conran had lengthy discussions with Don Ryder, Reed's chairman, and the firm prepared a detailed feasibility study with the aid of their accountants, advertising agency and marketing consultants. "We were really fired with tremendous enthusiasm", says Conran. "The thought of all the finance available from Reed, and their experience of the do-it-yourself market from their subsidiary

Wallpaper Manufacturers, wedded to the particular expertise of Habitat, was positively thrilling. We presented a five-year plan – the first we had ever made – to Reed, and they said they would give us their answer within a week. During that week they bought the International Publishing Corporation and told us they were very sorry, but they had enough on their plate already without taking on us as well, and could not go ahead. It was a very bitter blow indeed".

It was the bitterness of this blow that led, he realises now, to "a rather too quick decision, made on the rebound" in the following year, 1968, to merge with the stationery and office furnishing chain of Ryman. Ryman was a publicly owned company which had for some time been interested in Habitat, and Conran liked the chairman Desmond Ryman, who now approached him with the invitation "to merge our business with theirs – the term used when someone wants to take you over" as Conran puts it with a wry smile. Conran's turnover by this time was about £3.4 million, Ryman's £4 million, with profits of around £400,000 and £600,000 respectively. "Rymans was a glamour share on the stock market, they had a strong contract business and a good chain of retail outlets. It seemed like a good way of acquiring capital for Habitat's expansion", while for Ryman the advantages lay in updating its rather staid image by association with the modern, go-ahead Habitat. The merger duly took place, Conran becoming joint Chairman of the new firm of Ryman Conran, with a personal holding of twenty per cent of the combined business. The Ryman family had some forty per cent and the rest of the equity was held by the public. However, the honeymoon period was soon over, as Conran puts it, and it rapidly became apparent that there were irreconcilabale differences between the two firms, particularly in management style, Rymans being paternalistic and Conrans more democratic. Several senior Conran personnel left at this stage, not much liking the new style of the business.

On the financial front too, rifts began to develop. Ryman Conran took various opportunities to expand the office equipment side of the business by making several expensive acquisitions. The right thing for it to do, as Conran now concedes, but it meant channelling off funds he had hoped would come Habitat's way. Lupton Morton, a mail order house with a list of over a million names, was acquired in 1969 (it became the seed of Habitat's now flourishing mail order side) and Straker Bedser with a chain of retail shops the following year, but both were short of capital. Meanwhile Habitat "rather languished" and the Ryman brothers began to lose interest in it, though the joint firm built up between 1968 and 1970 from a combined turnover of around £7 million to about £16 million. "It taught me a great deal", says Conran, "about the workings of a large concern, being chairman of a public company with all the attendant involvement with the Stock Exchange, bankers and institutions". But Habitat was not expanding, in fact the balance sheet appeared to show it was making a loss, and after what Conran describes as "a lot of discussion and wrangling", he offered in 1970 to buy Habitat back out of the group, and this offer was accepted. In the event this proved harder to accomplish than he had anticipated. It was difficult to get a merchant bank to agree to put up the necessary funds, but he finally managed to re-possess it for around £650,000, keeping his Ryman shares as security for a loan; he put up £500,000 and Midland Montagu the remaining £150,000 of the equity. The contract was signed in June 1970 and although the company belonged technically to Conran from that date, (he only bought out the Habitat chain, leaving the factory at Thetford and the contract furnishing company with Ryman) the sale was not finalised until January 1971. "There was a six-month period in a sort of limbo", Conran recalls, "and during that limbo something very peculiar happened – when the accounts were disentangled it became evident that Habitat, which Rymans had thought was unprofitable, was extremely profitable, so the situation arose of Habitat actually lending money back to Ryman".

So it was in a confident and happy mood that Conran concluded his re-purchase of Habitat and, rejoined by several of his former management team, similarly overjoyed at this restoration, he set up Habitat Design Holdings to acquire the seven existing British stores. He moved his design group to studios in Neal Street, Covent Garden: the former managing director of the Thetford factory, Michael Tyson, became

managing director of the whole company, and a new financial director was appointed who was formerly with the
accountants Arthur Andersen.

The next two or three years was a period of rapid growth.
Habitat opened a series of new stores in the Midlands and
Southern England, and established a vast warehouse complex
at Wallingford which included a protected play area for
customers' children, with 'play sculptures' designed by
Eduardo Paolozzi. Conran Associates, the design group,
acquired some important contracts during this time, including work on two hotels in Jamaica for the Intercontinental
chain, and they designed their first range of products for
Airfix Industries under the trade name Crayonne. The
finances of the company were at last on a sound footing, and
one particular stroke of good fortune came Conran's way
when the Burton group decided to buy Rymans. Conran's
holding now turned out to be worth about £1.5 million,
and he quickly sold it, using the proceeds to fund the rapid
Habitat expansion. He also bought out Midland Montagu's
stake in the company, partly because they were unwilling
to agree with an employee share scheme which Conran had
long cherished and which, as described later, he was ultimately and successfully to put into operation.

It now became obvious that with expansion in the U.K.
consolidated, the next step should be into Europe. Conran
commissioned feasibility studies which showed that opportunities in France and Germany were more or less equal,
although West Germany had a higher per capita expenditure
on furniture. The company nonetheless decided on France,
largely because they had already designed many items for the
huge Prisunic chain store, had good relations with them and
were reasonably familiar with the French market through
this connection. Their first store in France, a very ambitious project, was opened at the Tour Montparnasse in
Paris in 1974, followed by a head office at Orgeval and
stores in Montpellier and Avenue Wagram in Paris and the
ill-fated Les Ullis, which was eventually closed after losing
almost £1 million. "We were trying out all the different
sorts of location", explains Conran, "city centre, out-of-
town, and the smallest town in which a Habitat store might

Wallingford — 80,000 sq. ft. of warehouse, showroom and head office.

Another view of the warehouse and loading bay.

be expected to be successful. But our opening in France coincided with the outbreak of the Arab-Israeli conflict and the price of oil rocketed, trade went into the doldrums and we were locked in to an expensive development plan. We expected to lose money, but we lost rather more than we bargained for".

Their English bankers at this time were Grindlays, who appeared with the firm in a television documentary "which we were stupid enough to make", showing how the current downturn in the economy and the property market in particular, was affecting their business. This had the unfortunate effect of panicking many Habitat suppliers who took the film, wrongly, as an indirect way of announcing the company was about to go bankrupt. Pressure was brought to bear by their own bankers for them to "stop the bleeding in France", and it was not an easy period for the firm. However, they came through, and the position across the channel was ameliorated by Conran Design Associates' success when they in turn opened a Paris office and obtained some prestigious contracts including the interior design of the new Centre Commerciale de la Defense, and later were retained by Renault. Stores have subsequently been opened in Brussels and Antwerp as well as other locations in France, there is a small mail order business with a French and Flemish language catalogue, and Conran currently has his sights set on West Germany, where he expects to open a test store in the autumn of 1981. "We are the only British retailer now properly profitable in France", remarks Conran, noting that the Tour Montparnasse store is particularly successful, it is one third smaller in area than the King's Road shop in London, but has twice the turnover.

There are few differences between one country and another in terms of lines stocked in the Habitat stores. Overall, eighty per cent of the 3,800 or so items the company sells are exclusive to them and made to their own design, (they no longer carry out any manufacture on their own account) and about fifteen to twenty per cent of merchandise is particular to each country. The Americans for example, use more table mats than the British and never use electric kettles; the French don't like lids on their saucepans and insist on all-cotton sheets, while a mixture of cotton and polyester or other man-made fibre is favoured by U.K. and American customers. "In any case, we don't believe in a great degree of centralisation," states Conran. "We want the French company, the Belgian, the British and the American to have local differences. It's set up a bit like a football league with a degree of competition, which benefits everybody".

There are both French and British buyers for each product category; furniture, lighting, textiles and floor coverings, china and glass, household linen, kitchen goods; and they frequently go together to trade fairs and exhibitions. Nationals of each country run the stores as far as possible. There are only two Britons in the U.S. company, one being Michael Tyson the managing director who went out to set up the American operation in 1976, and Habitat's policy of working as closely as possible with its suppliers and helping them to expand along with itself is followed as carefully overseas as it is in Britain. Both Marks & Spencer and Mothercare are cited by Conran as superlative examples of this attitude, and he can point to many firms who have flourished as a result of Habitat's custom, such as Sampsons, run by a man who used to work in the factory in Thetford, now major suppliers of pine furniture to the group, and a Swedish furniture manufacturer called Innovator who approached Conran with their designs some seven years ago. China, Denmark and India are now also major suppliers of merchandise. "This good relationship with our suppliers is a strong reason why we don't want to carry out any manufacture ourselves", explains Conran. "When a retail firm also has a factory of its own, suppliers tend to be wary and suspicious, unwilling to make a total commitment to you, because they always think you might switch orders to your own factory if circumstances change. Or if they come up with a certain new process, you might copy it. And it really is impossible to be both at once. The factory is always running at a different pace to the shops and you get continual problems either of over-supply or shortage.

When Michael Tyson and his colleagues went out to the United States to begin work on the feasibility study into the possibilities for Habitat across the Atlantic they decided the first step should be to try and build up a chain of between twenty and twenty-five stores in the North East of America, and any further expansion should be done by separate organisations set up specifically to operate on the West Coast, in the Mid-West, the "Sun-Belt" and so on. They felt that many other British retailers, whose efforts had not been noticeably successful in the American market, had made an elementary mistake in treating the whole operation as one large country, rather than areas with pronounced local differences, not so much in what they would buy but in the methods of merchandising.

Conran's, The Market, Citicorp Center, New York. 40,000 sq. ft. on two floors. Opened 1977.

Conran chose to open his first U.S. store in a brand new building, the Citicorp Center in New York. The firm did not have an easy introduction into the States, the first set-back being the discovery that they could not use the name Habitat.

It was one of the trade marks used by a furniture and lighting manufacturer and although about eighty other U.S. businesses trade under the Habitat name, they went to court to prevent Conran's new venture from doing so, on the grounds that it would provide unfair competition, and were successful. Other difficulties ensued from the choice of Citicorp itself. The fifty-nine storey building with a sloping roof (eighth tallest building in the world) was developed by the parent company of the American Citibank and is now a magnificent shopping centre, but because other prospective tenants were afraid it would not be finished on time they were slow to come forward and Conran's, for four months, was the only store open in an otherwise empty building — not a happy position for a retailer. Added to this they experienced a fire, some of the worst New York winter weather in living memory, and the non-arrival of all the Christmas stock because of a dock strike. However they successfully surmounted all these disasters, (although the U.S. company is not yet profitable, Conran estimates it will take altogether about four years) and have gone on to institute a mail order business there, operating from the firm's New Rochelle head office, and to sign contracts for five more stores in the North East including one in a converted tobacco warehouse in Georgetown, the most affluent and cosmopolitan area of Washington.

Conran's in New York benefits from the freedom to stay open seven days a week, which particularly pleases Terence Conran, a keen advocate of Sunday trading. In Britain the only Habitat stores able to trade on Sundays are in Glasgow and Edinburgh. No other store in the U.S. is emulating what Habitat is doing — selling, as they have done in this country, a 'total look' of furniture, fabrics and kitchenware. Furniture, made to Habitat design and specifications, is bought in the U.S. as are domestic textiles, while most other merchandise is imported and sold at prices which, although considerably higher than those in the U.K., are still low compared with Conran's U.S. competitors.

The finance for the U.S. venture, around £4 million altogether, was not forthcoming from the British banking system, although Conran tried first to raise the money in this country. "The British banks, even in 1976 and 1977 were still talking about us as if we were some trendy, fly-by-night business entirely dependent on fashion and might go out of business at any time. Most of them showed a complete lack of imagination, a lack of the capacity to understand a new idea". He found a different attitude in the Netherlands, however, where he experienced immediate sympathy with his aims from Bank Mees & Hope, a subsidiary of the giant Dutch Algemene Bank Nederland (A.B.N.) "They liked and understood what we were doing. To them it seemed a perfectly ordinary operation; a chain of stores selling household goods, a straightforward well-run business". With strong financial relationships in the States, Bank Mees & Hope proved an excellent banking partner for Habitat and have provided backing in this country and France as well as in America. "We have built up a close relationship with them, and they are so pleasant to deal with that I asked one of their directors to join our board, which has proved a most successful move. And it was done at our request, not theirs as is so often the case when a banker sits on the board of one of its client companies".

Discussion of the American operations brings Conran to the inevitable consideration of when or if, his company is likely to go public. "At the moment we are planning to do so early in the 1980s. We have demonstrated that we can make the French chain profitable, and we would like to demonstrate that we can do the same in America. Three successful and profitable businesses would make a good public launch". Asked if he has any misgivings about what must be a crucial turning point in the fortune of any company, and too, is often greeted with mixed feelings by the founder when he sees his own creation passing in some degree out of his hands, Conran is reflective. "I suppose in one way I would like it to be a public company. To go public seems to be a demonstration of one's success as a businessman, despite the misgivings and doubts expressed by so many people — retailers, bankers, institutions. We have made a success, and done some novel things like our Employee Share Scheme and our system of computerised stock control. It's the accolade of acceptability, but I certainly don't look forward with much enthusiasm to the problems of being chairman of a public company".

The Habitat profit-linked share plan is indeed new and has been implemented so successfully that Conran is now gratified to find other companies, "even Marks & Spencers!" have come to them for advice on starting up similar schemes, and since he initiated it some fifty or sixty large public companies have followed suit on behalf of their own employees. Conran himself consulted the John Lewis Partnership before he drew up his plans — "they were most generous with their advice" — but the Habitat scheme goes even further than the John Lewis one, which is confined to giving dividends to employees rather than shares, so when they leave the company they leave with nothing. "If you work for a capitalist organisation" says Conran, "I see no reason why you should not benefit and become a capitalist yourself. I think everyone should be able to own shares according to a ratio of their salary and the company's profitability, and we started to examine the whole position in the early 1970s, and actually launched the scheme in 1976.

Conran was emphatic at the time of the launch that none of the employees should see it as a gesture of "paternalistic generosity". He wanted everyone working for Habitat to feel fully involved with the company, and this he felt was only possible if they were shareholders. There was a good deal of necessary preliminary work with the Inland Revenue to be done, and agreement from the unions, whose initial attitude was ambivalent, to be obtained. Shop assistants are not unionised, but some of the transport and warehouse staff are members of T.G.W.U. Employees become shareholders after one full financial year with the company, and at no cost to themselves. A proportion of the profits each year are used to pay for an allocation of shares to new and existing shareholders — the first allocation, in 1976, was of £143,000 at a share price of 25p. After three years the shares become the full property of the holders, (if the holder leaves the group before the three years are up, they have to be returned to the trust set up specifically to administer the fund) after which a limited internal market operates so that those who wish can sell back their shares for cash to the trust, which is composed of an outside solicitor, the

Habitat financial director Ian Peacock and an elected employee. The worth of the shares is audited each year and at the latest valuation in Autumn '78 the original 25p share stood at 90p, so some of the employees, particularly those who benefited from the special long service allocation when the scheme was launched and have participated in each of the subsequent annual distributions, are now in possession of healthy nest-eggs worth several thousand pounds. Conran himself, who at one time owned one hundred per cent of Habitat, now holds seventy-three per cent, with the remaining twenty-seven per cent being mainly held either directly or in trust for past and present employees. About fifty per cent of the staff have been allocated shares, and Conran sees signs that turnover of personnel is beginning to drop as loyalty and a feeling of commitment are increased by the ownership of shares in their own company — an additional bonus. The staff turnover problem is always a major headache for retailers and Habitat has been no exception, spending large sums of money on training, a wasted investment if the person concerned then promptly leaves.

Each employee joining the retail side of the business takes part in a training programme designed not only to provide him with the specific knowledge and skill for his particular job, whether sales assistant, clerical worker or warehouse operative but, (which the company views as even more important) to instil in him the principles of 'creative retailing' on which Habitat prides itself and which is at the root of Conran's business philosophy. These training programmes are carried on throughout all countries in which they operate — in France Habitat spends twenty per cent more than the statutory national requirement on training — and in Britain its efforts were marked in 1979 by an award from the Government sponsored Distributive Industry Training Board. Recent developments have included the establishment of a three-year management succession plan with a trainee scheme for floor managers, half-hour weekly training sessions in the stores and the introduction of a new audio-visual training scheme.

Special emphasis is placed on familiarity with Habitat's

vast range of products and great use is made of the crisply produced catalogue. The first catalogue was published soon after the merger with Ryman and acquisition of Lupton Morton, and for some years was distributed free, later a charge, currently 65p, was introduced in order to "get the catalogues in the right hands" and just under a million of them are sold annually, costing somewhat more than the cover price to produce. These catalogues constitute one of the company's main marketing tools – 600,000 are published in this country, 300,000 in Europe and 100,000 in the U.S. (where the number will be increased this year) and mail order now accounts for some five per cent of group turnover. There are also the enormously successful *House Book, Kitchen Book* and *Bed and Bath Book*, massive encyclopaedias of living styles and information about all aspects of decorating and equipping the home. Edited by Conran himself and designed by Conran Associates, the books are published by Mitchell Beazley in Britain and are also produced in the U.S.A., France, Belgium, Spain, Holland, Australia and New Zealand. Other publications with which the firm is closely involved include an annual *Cook's Diary*, a *Gardener's Diary* and innumerable other catalogues and brochures for clients of the design group such as Crayonne, Levi Strauss and the Electricity Council.

The innovatory till and stock control system which Habitat has recently put in is controlled by a Burroughs computer, with tills from the U.S. company, Data Terminal Systems, plus various other bits of 'hardware'. The £1.5 million installation proved something of a nightmare, Conran says, because Habitat was a guinea pig for the scheme. Every item sold by the firm is identified by a code number, and when this is rung up on the till its current price is shown automatically, thus doing away with the tedious chore of pricing each item separately – only the shelves carrying prices. Details of each individual sale are stored in the till's memory and transmitted at night to the central computer via the Post Office land lines, where they are processed in a variety of ways to give a breakdown into sales analyses for the buyers, lists for re-ordering and delivery and so on. The teething troubles arose from the fact that the necessary

The 1979 'Housebook'

Kitchen utensils designed by Conran Associates for Boots.

chip for the memory of all items was not ready at the time Habitat bought the system, although they were not told this, and neither had it been tested on the European tele-communication system. "It cost us a fortune in lost data and incorrect stock control, as we had already abandoned our old N.C.R. and Sweda till system" says Conran, adding that just as Habitat got it working satisfactorily, I.B.M. announced that they would bring out an integrated package which would have been far simpler to install; but he feels in the long run it will prove very valuable. Another recent development is the Habitat Credit Card which is funded by Barclaycare, the finance and administration section of Barclaycard, who have, in the year they have been operating individual credit card schemes for retailers, set them up for a number of other stores such as Debenhams and International Stores.

As well as the Habitat stores and Conran stores in the U.S. Terence Conran also owns The Conran Shop in the Fulham Road (on the site of the first Habitat shop) which specialises in a collection of more expensive and individual designs in home furnishings and antiques (currently including a range of traditional chestnut furniture from the Dordogne where Conran has a holiday house) and such items as handmade Orrefors glass. The Conran shop works closely with Conran Associates, his design team, which is now the largest in the E.E.C. with a turnover in 1978/79 of nearly £1.6 million. The team is about eighty strong, including those based in Paris, with its headquarters in Neal Street, Covent Garden (next to the Neal Street restaurant which Conran also owns — an expression of his love and knowledge of good food). About eighteen per cent of their work is done for Habitat itself, for whom they produce the annual catalogue and carry out a continual programme of new store design and develop-ment. They also have a wide spectrum of other clients for whom they have created a myriad of designs; packaging for International Stores and Sainsburys, housewares for Boots, Timothy Whites, Woolworths and Marks & Spencer. Com-plete stores for Andre Simon, Interio (Switzerland) and de Bijenkorf (Holland), display systems for Levi Strauss and Rynians; and offices for a host of clients including adverti-sing agencies (Ogilvy Benson and Mather, McCormick

Richards) and the editor of the Sunday Times; the design of
1.5 million square feet of La Defense, the commercial centre
to the west of Paris, due to open in 1980, and product
design for Renault (France). Most of the group's income
still derives from interior design work, but they have concentrated on developing the product and graphic design
departments, and some thirty per cent of their work is done
abroad.

Contract furnishing, with which Conran has been associated
almost from his earliest days, is still a flourishing area of the
company, and in 1978 Habitat Contracts came up with a
particularly novel idea in the 'Housepack' — a complete
package containing all the basic essentials to furnish a one,
two or three bedroomed house, from beds tables and chairs
right down to teaspoons. Since its introduction they have
sold one hundred and ninety-nine at an average price of
£2,500, mostly to the Middle East, but some as far afield as
Hong Kong and Nigeria. A few were even sold in Britain,
although they are primarily designed for site houses, and they
have been bought by such customers as British Airways,
Massey Ferguson, Price Waterhouse and Racal Telecommuni-
cations. In Libya a film company used them to house actors
Anthony Quinn and Oliver Reed while they were filming
"*Omar Mukhtar*". The housepacks are designed to fit into
standard sea containers, and an additional attraction is that
the selling company handles all necessary export documen-
tation.

Conran's intense concern with design, the very root of
his business philosophy, has been transmitted to the people
who work with him and who find his boundless energy and
enthusiasm a source of excitement and inspiration, even if
it sometimes infuriates them. He frankly admits to out-
bursts of temperament, using his temper to "stir the blood"
of his designers. "I hate the dull pattern of sanity", and his
colleagues confess they are never sure whether he will love a
new idea or hate it. What they are certain of is that he lives
almost entirely for Habitat. He detests waste of any kind,
whether of money, ideas or time, and his own time is filled
with a fearsome programme of work involving extensive
overseas travel, not only seeing shops and suppliers and

Tenth annual Habitat U.K. Catalogue. 650,000 sold on the bookstalls alone.

customers of the design group, but also selecting new sites; "Enormously important, and for every site we buy, we have probably viewed at least three or four possible alternatives" all of which he visits personally. His eye for detail is legendary; "reports, brochures, computer print-outs, are all carefully checked by experts, then who picks out the error? Terence!" exclaims one of the directors of Habitat Designs.

The company has received many awards. They have twice won the Royal Society of Arts Duke of Edinburgh Award for Design Management, for example, and the Wallingford headquarters has won three architectural honours — the Financial Times Award, the Structural Steel Design Award and the Architectural Heritage Year Award. Conran himself is a member of the Advisory Council of the Victoria and Albert Museum and the Council of the Royal College of Art. Yet his approach to designs remains completely unacademic, tough and uncompromising, soundly rooted in his practical experience as a retailer; a position he views as "the real creative force in marketing in the future", the retailer being able to "experiment economically, study the results efficiently and put his findings into effect immediately". Certainly his own retailing efforts have been outstandingly creative and his own designs have, within a few short years, undoubtedly changed the way people live.

GERALD RONSON
Leading from the Front

Gerald Ronson at forty has already worked more hours than most men of sixty-five; he revels in a punishing fifteen hours a day, six or six and a half days a week. He believes it is almost entirely due to his capacity for hard work that he has built up Heron Corporation Ltd. to its present size as Britain's second largest privately owned company (only outstripped by the Littlewood retail chain). Since the Holding Company was formed in 1965 it has had an unbroken succession of profit increases each year, rising from a pre-tax profit of £104,000 in 1965 to £8.2 million in 1978-79, and the group's net worth had increased in those fourteen years from £1.5 million to £70 million, internally generated with no issue of equity capital. Today Heron operates in a wide range of businesses in the fields of property, housebuilding, petrol retailing, insurance, motor and motorcycle distribution and consumer products.

Ronson left school at fifteen − "as soon as I legally could" − and after taking a business course at Clark's College went into the family furniture business started by his father, Henry Ronson, (hence the name He-ron) the son of Russian emigre parents. Ronson is careful to point out that his is no rags to riches story. The furniture business, with a turnover of three quarters of a million pounds and employing over 200 people to make dining chairs and tables, was obviously a success.

He always enjoyed visiting the factory, and when only twelve used to go down and help out on Saturday mornings, longing to put formal education behind him and get on with his true love — business. He worked in every department from the sawdust of the mill to fitting, polishing and cabinet-making. By the time he was eighteen he was works manager, "because I was capable of it". It was his first taste of management and he relished it.

However, the late fifties were difficult times for the British furniture trade. Scandinavian imports were then fashionable, and the three major retailers had a stranglehold on manufacturers, cutting margins ruthlessly and often insisting on up to a year's credit. It was a struggle for manufacturers to make a return of even four per cent. The unions were making determined efforts to organise the workers and Henry Ronson decided he had had enough; also he did not welcome the idea of Gerald and his younger son, Laurence, spending their lives in the furniture trade. So, despite Gerald's disappointment at losing his newly-won managerial status, he decided to sell up at the end of 1956 and put the proceeds into a property business, taking his son into fifty-fifty partnership with him. They started, "with little or no experience" recalls Ronson, at the beginning of the following year. According to his son, Ronson senior thought it would be an easier way to make money, with fewer headaches.

Even in those days there were many restrictions. Since 1947 there have been planning controls of varying degrees of severity in force, administered by local government; industrial development certificates going hand in hand with regional incentives operated by a system of grants and allowances, together with countless rules and regulations covering the actual building operations once permission was granted to build at all. It was excellent experience for the Ronsons, who started out by building small, medium-priced houses — around one hundred and fifty a year — and as the property boom began to take off, they followed up by developing office buildings, shopping centres and larger and larger scale commercial ventures.

The first houses were built in the home counties, and Hoddesden north of London and Nuneaton were among their early city-centre developments. In Hoddesden, on a four-acre site, ninety per cent of the shopping centre was let before completion, which is typical of most of Ronson's property ventures. The business leapt ahead as they built houses to provide homes for people working in the new shops, offices and factories. Gerald Ronson's younger brother, Laurence, is now Managing Director of the Corporation's housing estate development division, which built about one thousand new homes last year. They concentrated in the south west, particularly the Bristol and Gloucester overspill areas and are now the largest housing estate developers in the west country. In 1970 they bought their largest competitor, the building firm of Stanshawe Estates.

Back to the 1960s, and the company was just getting up "a good head of steam" as Ronson puts it, when the newly elected Labour government in 1964 dealt them what seemed like a body blow. George Brown (now Lord George-Brown) introduced, at the end of the year, controls on commercial building that staggered the property world. First, in November, came the announcement of a standstill on all new office developments in the Greater London Council and Metropolitan areas. This was followed the next month by the Control of Offices and Industrial Development Bill, which required new offices to have, as well as normal planning permission, Office Development Certificates from the Board of Trade for both new building and change of use. Controls were particularly stringent in the Greater London area, where virtually no permits were granted except in very special circumstances. Factory development was affected by the new powers allowing the limits below which industrial development certificates were not required to be varied.

As it turned out a good many developers benefitted from these regulations, which created such a shortage of office space that they could let properties which had been standing vacant for months or years during the earlier period of over-supply. Poorly drafted Parliamentary Bills so often seem to achieve the opposite of what was intended. However, few could have seen this result, and for the Ronsons the 1964 restrictions posed a crucial question; "which way to go now as a company?" The way Ronson chose was to

71

most outsiders and even to many close to him, absolutely amazing. He went into gasoline. "Everyone said I was mad, but to me it seemed obvious".

Taking on major oil companies at the highly specialised, fiercely competitive business of service station operation certainly looked like a mug's game. However, Ronson, with his characteristic caution, did a thorough preliminary investigation before committing himself, including a tour of the United States, which confirmed him in his conviction. He saw interest rates rising and knew the era of easy profits was coming to an end, particularly in the property business. It was time to diversify. He always loved cars − he now drives a Rolls Royce, but at this time Lamborghinis were his special love − and this led him naturally towards marketing petrol and oil. Perhaps the most significant reason for his choice was his recognition of the key point that selling petrol was predominantly a real estate operation; sites cost on average ten times as much as the installations.

Ronson opened his first service station at Marshalswick, St. Albans in Hertfordshire in April 1966, and he proceeded to turn on their heads the traditional ideas about petrol retailing. Some twenty per cent of petrol stations were being run by independent small businessmen who rented sites from major oil companies, the rest being owned by dealers. Ronson's plan was to centralise the operation, relying on close budgetary control, staff supervision and above all discipline and service on the forecourt.

Gerald Ronson is a born salesman, and his marketing flair − genius might not be too strong a word, though he would deny this − was now given full scope for the first time. The stations were heavily splashed in the local press before their opening, and Ronson in the early days practised a savage price-cutting policy, selling petrol at fivepence a gallon less than his competitors. This gave rise to malicious current rumours that he was buying supplies from behind the Iron Curtain, but the source was less exotic; U.S. Phillips Petroleum at first and later Signal Oil and Gas, called VIP in this country.

He concentrated especially on the London area − having observed that fifty per cent of petrol sold in Britain was within a fifty-mile radius of the capital — and applied his keen 'nose' for prime sites, which he had already used to good effect in the property market, to selecting equally profitable sites for his new service stations. They were not easy to find, even in the mid-60s, because it was so difficult to get permission to build a new one, and still is — there are probably not a dozen 'virgin site' planning consents given for filling stations in the south of England in a year — the whole country by American standards has remarkably few stations. His years in the property business were invaluable to him when it came to getting the planning permits necessary even if you want to knock down and rebuild; eighteen months waiting for the go-ahead is not uncommon. Ronson drove thousands of miles a year round Britain looking for possible sites, until "roads were coming up in my face" as he described it later.

The Heron property business was not sold off to finance this new venture. The service stations were financed by borrowed money. Two large pension funds which had previously lent money to Heron agreed to enter a sale and leaseback arrangement with Ronson for the sum of £1 million. This large amount of cash enabled Ronson to standardise all his filling stations as far as possible, right from the start, rather as McDonalds do for hamburgers. The sites were razed to the ground and entirely rebuilt. "We put our image on the site, and we don't cheat in construction".

An important part of that image was service. Ronson claims to have introduced the world's first self-service stations at the end of 1966, but in any case the standards of forecourt service he offered his customers were far above the usually indifferent performance of the major oil companies. Immaculate lavatories — pink for ladies, blue for men — windscreen washed without asking, high-speed automatic cut-off pumps, guaranteed octane rates, four tyres for the price of three, free oil change (you only paid for the oil, not the labour), were some of the baits which he used, with increasing success, to lure customers into his stations. Once there, they could pay by cheque, Barclaycard or Diners Club card — which was certainly not possible on most competitive sites.

Obviously, all this took intensive training, and was expensive (still is) for the company. But Ronson does not grudge the cost. He instituted a system of supervisors, one per twelve stations, and by 1972 was spending over £70,000 a year on training them. On top of this, he started his own by now famous weekend spot checks on stations throughout the country. He spends at least forty Saturdays a year, sometimes Christmas Day as well, on the road from 7 a.m. until 7.30 p.m. calling on as many as twenty-five stations in a day. "I know their staffing problems. I know how hard they work". He travels between 60,000 and 70,000 miles a year in this country, as he feels this is vital to a thriving business. His philosophy is: "you must have a leader and a captain, and he must lead from the front. It's no good just sitting behind your desk, you've got to get out, be approachable, and don't ask people to work harder than you do yourself, to work more hours than you do".

These aggressive marketing techniques developed as more service stations were added. Ronson was a great believer in trading stamps — "Quad Stamps!" often screamed from the sites — and he soon introduced Heron Gold Stamps, free offers such as glasses and china, and subsequently Heron Autoshops stocking as many as 1,000 items. "Selling petrol is just like selling toffee apples" he remarked.

In spite of woeful predictions when he started, and an operating loss of around £70,000 in the first year, the service stations began to pay. By 1968 there were thirty-five within a fifty-mile radius of London and by 1972 Heron was opening a new one every ten days. Workshops and showrooms were sublet to outside tenants, while Heron concentrated on keeping the sites scrupulously clean, and above all selling petrol and oil. They reached maximum sales levels in three years, it usually takes five years) and achieved eighty per cent of the business in their first year. Soon Heron could triumphantly claim that gallonage from their sites was seven times the national average.

Ronson soon abandoned his early price-cutting policies in favour of a more flexible system based on local prices. By 1967 he abolished price-cutting altogether as the major oil companies had embarked on a 'price war' which finally ground to a halt at about this time. By now his competitors were distinctly uneasy; the new boy, with all the dice loaded against him, had survived in the petrol jungle and was obviously here to stay.

In 1968, the Shell Mex and B.P. marketing unit offered to buy him out, but Ronson, who had already had similar approaches from at least five other British and U.S. petrol companies, had other plans. He profitably sold off a certain number of the stations, agreeing to continue operating them for a period of seven years, and simultaneously negotiated a twenty-year development loan at preferential interest rates. The price realised for these stations was boosted by the Government's action in lifting restrictions on company-owned sites. He proceeded to invest the loan in more petrol stations, so that after selling thirty-five sites for a seven figure sum in 1968, he was able to sell Texaco twice as many, on similar terms eighteen months later and in this way he generated £70 million by 1978. Big oil companies, just like breweries, appreciate sites with a potentially high turnover, and "we taught the wholesalers how to become retailers". Heron has continued this policy with highly satisfactory results up to the present day, and there seems no reason to suppose it will be dropped. A couple of years ago it was estimated that the Corporation had a guaranteed cash flow of around £5 million a year over the next few years from this process of service station purchase sale and loan. And this did not include the other sides of the business.

"It is gratifying", says Ronson, "that Heron is known as a petrol company — but that represents only ten per cent of the Corporation's net worth. But it's made the rest possible". His policy has been to use the petrol stations as 'pumps' to prime a constant stream of cash towards the investment in new sites; "you've got to have the whole concept properly balanced, develop a cash flow and be in a healthy position to meet the interest on property loans".

The property side of the Corporation grew in parallel with the service stations. Up until the general property 'crash' of 1975 there was plenty of money available for developers, particularly from the secondary banks, who in many cases caused their own downfall by getting too deeply involved with property. Ronson, however, has never used the facilities of fringe financial companies, always banking with the 'Big Four' joint stock banks, and throughout his business life liquidity has been the main tenet of the Corporation's policy.

In 1965 at the age of 26, Ronson was being widely spoken of and written about as Britain's 'youngest millionaire'. In January that year Heron issued a £2.8 million twenty year quoted debenture stock with a seven per cent coupon handled by M. Samuel & Co. and brokers Joseph Sebag — not an easy thing to place for an unquoted property company, but it was extremely successful, for the City realised the security, a "nice selection of freehold and leasehold properties" was good. The City and Ronson have a healthy respect for each other, and Ronson's close links with old-established companies like Samuel and Sebag were an advantage, especially in the early days when some of his competitors were not above trying to take advantage of his youth. "But because we are a private company, with our ordinary shares unquoted, it gives us much more flexibility; we are not answerable to the institutions, and we don't have to kowtow in any way to the City".

Right from his first property deal, Ronson set his sights on Europe. He understood the implications of Britain's approach to membership of the E.E.C., and in 1967 took his first momentous step into Europe when estate agents Richard Ellis introduced him to a development opportunity in the rue de la Paix in Paris. After long and complex negotiations he acquired the site from Caron Perfumes and the building was completed in 1971. Often quoted as one of the most successful developments ever completed by a British developer overseas, the Heron building of 44,000 square feet in the prestigious 1st Arrondissement had no difficulty finding blue chip tenants such as I.B.M., National Westminster and Mexican Airlines, with rents starting at the equivalent of £8 per square foot, tied to an index linked with inflation to protect the landlord. While not underestimating the difficulties of the negotiations, Ronson enjoyed certain aspects of them — "when you talk money to a Frenchman, he listens" — and he appreciated, as many less successful competitiors failed to do, the great difference across the channel in the attitudes and practices of banks, stock market and investors. The £2.5 million development of No. 10 rue de la Paix (a former town house of the Bugatti family) was the forerunner of a hefty European property development programme, embracing properties in France, Spain, Switzerland, Germany and Belgium. They are all prime commercial properties in excellent sites in the main commercial centres, chosen and developed on the same well-tried principles which Ronson has successfully used in the U.K.

These great bastions at home and abroad saved Heron from disaster in the dark days of 1975 and 1976 when the property boom in the U.K. came to an abrupt halt. The collapse has been well documented; the downfall of some of the 'pushers' — companies borrowing short for long

A Heron development of 160,000 sq. ft. in Albert Square, Manchester.

term projects – rising interest rates and the beginnings of the secondary bank failures referred to earlier. The Community Land Act took some of the initiative away from developers and gave it to local authorities, and by the beginning of 1976 there was, to all intents and purposes, a complete stoppage in office development in the urban centres and hardly any new shops and factories. The country was plunging into economic recession and government encouraged offices to be re-located outside London, where 'To Let' boards sprang up like mushrooms overnight, rents began to tumble and rates and service charges soared.

Heron, unlike many other developers, survived this critical time, largely because the Ronson team had never taken their eyes off those twin essentials, cash flow and liquidity, which others in the heady days of the early 1970s had clearly either forgotten or neglected. Even at the lowest, their interest coverage with the banks was always between one and a half and two times; "it gave confidence to the banks" as Ronson puts it; they never lost their nerve. A lot of properties have been sold since completion, but never below book value and thus they retained their financial strength.

Just as Ronson carries on his unceasing round of inspection in Britain, so he travels increasingly overseas, doing some 80,000 miles a year in Europe, the United States and the Far East. He spends about one week in six in the States, and has set aside at least £10 million for the expansion across the Atlantic which he is determined to carry through over the next decade.

"Ideally, I would like to have a third of the Corporation's assets in America by 1987" says Ronson, who views the U.S. as the "last true bastion of capitalism". He doesn't intend, however, to run service stations or car sales, recognising the difficulties of operating highly competitive and labour intensive concerns at a distance of several thousand miles. Rather, he has decided on property, insurance companies, and savings and loan associations. These are doubly attractive by reason of the sophisticated and experienced management which can operate without day-to-day assistance from Heron, plus the fact that such businesses are subject in the U.S. to government regulation and control; "that's double protection for a foreign investor. You can rest easier at night knowing someone from the government is watching your operations".

Just as in Britain he has relied on the expertise of proven companies such as Barclays Merchant Bank, Hill Samuel, Joseph Sebag and Richard Ellis, so Ronson has a formidable team of advisers in the States, consisting of Salomon Brothers, Price Waterhouse & Co. and Cravath, Swaine & Moore. And his cautious approach to propositions in Europe, the patient, painstaking attention to detail which has characterised all his deals, will certainly be followed in the U.S. "I'm not rushing to come back with something, like a woman out shopping", as he remarked to an American interviewer from Forbes business magazine.

Nevertheless, he can move at full speed when he thinks the time is right, and the British property world is familiar with such stories as his purchase of a site for a block of flats in St. John's Wood on the same day he spotted the 'For Sale' notice going up as he drove to work in the morning. He has the nose to scent out property, as he says, and because the company is still privately owned he is able to say yes or no immediately, although such swift decisions are rare.

In 1970 Ronson bought the London based Rolls Royce distributorship of H.R. Owen from the Lex Service Group for over £1 million. It was run by an old friend of his, Peter Reynolds, and when he told Ronson it had been taken over, but Rolls Royce had blocked the deal, Ronson stepped in and with Rolls' approval bought it. Two years later, by a reverse takeover he acquired seventy per cent of Scottish Automobile as a natural extension of Heron's oil and growing motor interests. This formed the nucleus of the Corporation's motor distribution activities, now known as the Heron Motor Group, with Reynolds as Chief Executive and Angus Grossart as Chairman.

Another acquisition in an associated field was the purchase of Suzuki (Great Britain) Ltd. in 1975. The Managing Director and controlling shareholder, Peter J. Agg, took the initiative and approached Ronson saying he thought his business would fit in well with the Heron style of management — "as indeed it has" confirms Ronson. The price paid was not disclosed but it was making at the time a turnover of around £11 million and supplied 650 dealers. Its management was left pretty well undisturbed after the purchase, Agg remaining "guv'nor in his own right" as Ronson describes him, and Suzuki's turnover more than doubled in the first year of Heron's ownership while it substantially increased its market share.

A sizeable stake of some twenty-six per cent in Henleys the car dealers, was bought in 1976 for just under £2 million, but sold off a year later to North West Securities, the H.P. subsidiary of the Bank of Scotland. "We are not building up an empire for its own sake", Ronson pointed out at the time of the sale, "we are out to make a profit. We have doubled our money on this investment". (In fact he did better and sold his stake for over £4 million).

Today, in 1979, the Corporation owns sixty-seven per cent of the Motor Group's shares, and it is the only part of Heron which is a publicly quoted company. Its profits have risen in the five years from 1974 to 1979 from £400,000 to £3 million, and net worth of the group within the same period has increased from £7 million to £22 million. In July of 1979 the Group announced turnover up thirteen per cent over the previous year and new car sales up ten per cent to 13,000 units as the Austin Morris range became more readily available. The Group deals mainly in Rolls Royce cars and Leyland cars and trucks, but does trade with other manufacturers and has recently opened its first Peugeot depot at Halesowen in the Midlands, as well as closely examining the whole depot network to judge the possibilities of adding other non-B.L. franchises in areas where British Leyland competition is strong. In 1978-79 the Group closed three out of nine commercial vehicle centres, which were making losses. The Heron Motor Group is also the U.K.'s second biggest Rolls Royce dealer, with profits stemming from the shortage of new models which makes for high trade-in values. All this profitability has not gone unnoticed by outsiders, and a recent approach (reputedly from Lonrho) was made by a bidder who obviously shared Ronson's own view that the current stock market price of 58p per share was greatly undervalued. Whatever was offered (and it was reported that

Ronson valued the company at £26 million or 70p per share) it was unsuccessful, and Ronson finds such negotiations tiresome. On this occasion he even threatened to return the Motor Group to private company status if he gets any similar 'irritations'. The main reason for his anger is that such episodes upset the Group's 2,500 or so staff. "We are very loyal to our staff here", he says, and makes it clear that any takeover would have to be in their best interests.

In spite of the slump, property deals continued to be the mainstay of the Corporation's activities in the 1970s. "The root of everything I do is in real estate, whether it is used as offices, or to sell motor cars, petrol or anything else". In 1972 Ronson joined a fifty-fifty partnership with Great Universal Stores in a £14 million development scheme for a site in Paris at Montparnasse, strategically placed near the Metro station and road to Orly airport. Financed by Credit Lyonnais, the plans included 200,000 square feet of offices and parking for 400 cars, and was said to be the largest of its kind ever undertaken in the French capital by a British firm. The following year Ronson bought the Figaro site at the Rond Point in the Champs Elysees after two years of intense negotiations with the owner, Madame Francoise Coty, widow of the French perfume manufacturer. The price was said to be about £9 to £10 million, and Heron own the site jointly with British merchant bankers Keyser Ullman and Union des Assurances de Paris, the largest state-owned French insurance company. The £40 million plan for development of this prime site is lavish. The upper floors will house ultra-modern offices, with two lower levels of shops (a total of 3,100 square metres) and two restaurants in a luxurious arcade and the whole building stands on the sunny side of one of the most famous streets in Europe, along which some 120,000 pedestrians pass every day.

The solidity of Heron's European property deals has shielded them from the hostilities and difficulties experienced abroad by some of their British competitors. However, Ronson does not under-estimate the complexities of buying overseas, but he is patient and cautious. Quite different from those whom he calls the "jump in, jump out merchants" out to make a quick profit, and whose activities, particularly in the early 1970s, attracted a good deal of opprobrium, and caused the countries concerned to threaten controls on development from overseas.

The Spanish property market is probably even more difficult than the French, but here again, to the envy of his rivals, Ronson has made a success. His first venture was in Madrid, where he completed a 95,000 square foot development in the Paseo de la Castellana in 1975. It was let immediately to blue chip tenants such as I.B.M., Banco Arabe Espanole and Societe Generale de Banque en Espagne, and has since proved to be one of the finest investments in the city. One feature of the Spanish property market causing difficulties for foreign investors is the government clampdown on 'open market' rentals; tenants sign leases on a three-year basis, rent rises are indexed to a cost of living calculation published monthly by the Instituto Nacional de Estadistica, and if tenants re-sign at the end of the three-year period rents cannot go up to open market levels. So investors tend to look for tenants in multi-tenanted buildings who will want to expand, this being the only opportunity for rental growth. This has led to a situation where buildings sold with vacant possession in major Spanish centres command twice the price of those fully let. The exact opposite of the position in the rest of Europe and North America.

In 1979, Heron purchased the troubled Interland Estates, which was in financial difficulties as a result of the 1974 property collapse. While part of its attraction was its tax credits, reputed to be some £10 million, it also conveniently fitted in with Heron's current portfolio, bringing in around fifteen sites in Britain which had taken seven years to assemble – five of them particularly good, in Covent Garden in Central London, in Harrow, in Richmond and two in Leeds, all with planning permission. Most of Interland's portfolio is for office development, and this purchase enables Heron to carry out a major building programme at a time when most developers are frantically searching for suitable land.

Apart from property, petrol and motor interests, Ronson has gone into two other main areas, consumer products and insurance. "I had the opportunity to buy Ingersoll and thought the name had potential, and it had a reasonable marketing organisation", says Ronson, who acquired a controlling interest in this seventy-five year old British watch distributor (third largest in the U.K.) for about £1 million in 1976, and he is pleased with its progress in the three years he has owned it. There was some competition to buy it from Hong Kong, (ninety per cent of its products come from the Far East) but Ronson, seeing a strong possibility of increasing its production of watches and clocks (twenty per cent of them quartz) by about a third, reputedly put £500,000 into promotion and into capital expenditure, as well as completely re-organising the sales force. This acquisition also added a cutlery company, Butlers of Sheffield, who make table cutlery, scissors and knives. This company has also benefited from an injection of capital for new machinery and the recent purchase of an adjoining factory into which to expand. The consumer products division has also expanded its range to include various other electronic items such as radios and TV games.

The Heron Corporation in 1977 bought the whole of the issued share capital of The National Insurance and Guarantee Corporation Ltd., an eighty-year-old insurance company which had a premium income of around £20 million per annum at the time of its purchase. It represents a natural extension of the group's motor interests, since it specialises in motor vehicle insurance which represents some eighty-five per cent of its business. Ronson now plans to develop the non-motor insurance side. "They were a bit wary of Heron at first", he recalls, "they thought we were going to turn them inside out. They were an old-established company with a first-class management team and the exposure to Heron has given them motivation and incentives – an injection of our philosophy – and it's worked out extremely well"; its profits doubled in the first year of Heron ownership. Offers for the Bourne and Hollingsworth retail store, and Halfords, the motor accessory, retail and distribution group, were made recently but came to nothing, though they gave the stock market some moments of excitement.

The Heron Corporation today is organised in seven divisions: petrol retailing, motor vehicle distribution and retailing, motorcycle distribution, housing estate development, consumer products, commercial property and insurance. Ronson sees it pushing into 1980 by means of a three-pronged attack on the separate fronts of property, Heron Trading (petrol, motors, Suzuki and consumer goods) and insurance.

Gerald Ronson with H.R.H. The Prince of Wales at the ceremony to mark the laying of the foundation stone at St. David's centre Cardiff.

"We're already a substantial company — with turnover around £400 million in 1979/80, and by 1981 we may well reach £500 million. The last three years we have been consolidating, and developing business management. We've got a lot of bright young men anxious to prove themselves, and it's an exciting period. Any company that has lived, as we have, through the last seven years from 1972, can expect to see great things. We have a five-year corporate plan on a rolling basis, updated every six months", explains Ronson, and he emphasises that his experience in the past difficult years has highlighted the necessity for tight financial controls. He is also particularly interested in the development of second-line management.

"I'm quite clear in my mind which way we are going over the next five years. We will make a major drive in the U.S. for the next two; but one has to go carefully, learn the market; it will take at least eighteen months to structure. You can see three phases in the growth of a large company — the first, generating wealth, we have already come through. The second is the one we are in now, development and consolidation. Thirdly, in perhaps ten years' time, I see Heron as a finance-oriented and real estate business. At the moment our assets are roughly two thirds in the U.K. and one third in Europe. The ideal situation by 1987 would be one third each in the U.K., the U.S.A. and Europe".

The financial strength and status of an organisation of this size are emphasised by three recent loans which Heron Corporation negotiated. A £17 million borrowing facility was announced in February 1978 with a consortium of the 'Big Four' clearing banks. It was an eight-year, secured loan, fifty per cent in sterling and fifty per cent in eurocurrency, with an undisclosed coupon which Ronson pronounced as "very acceptable". It was designated for re-finance of existing borrowing on U.K. properties, which were thus fully funded on either medium or long term bases at a satisfactory interest rate. Similarly, a ten-year, 4¼ per cent unsecured loan of 35 million Swiss Francs was raised on the Swiss stock market in January 1979, and the proceeds used to repay an existing 6¾ per cent loan of 30 million Swiss Francs. Ronson has also had a $25 million loan facility arranged since the spring of 1979 allowing him to close quickly on any likely opportunity which may arise in the U.S.

Talking to Ronson in his panelled, comfortable but not obviously opulent fourth floor office in the Corporation's Marylebone headquarters is an invigorating experience. He speaks quickly and decisively, listens attentively, answers questions briskly and to the point — and frankly. This candid manner is reflected in the openness which he has always shown in business. The Corporation does not go out of its way to court publicity, but is usually ready to answer reasonable questions as to its activities and intentions (not always a characteristic of large, privately owned firms). The speed with which he talks and thinks gives the clue to how he manages to cope with his demanding schedule, and there are hundreds of stories testifying to his energy and hard work. One for instance, often told by a banker returning from Paris on the last flight on Saturday, who offered Ronson a lift home, to be met by a courteous but firm refusal; Ronson was going straight to his office to work. "My wife knows the way I work; she understood my work programme before we were married, and the children are used to it", claims Ronson, the father of four daughters. He does concede, however, that he does not spend enough time with his family, though "when I do go home, I switch off. Home is home and business is business". He loves fast cars and boats, both of which are partly business. Heron also own a yacht building company, Heron Marine.

Among other commitments, the Heron Corporation is currently developing a site in the centre of Glasgow and, together with a consortium of four leading British retailers, a mammoth £30 million city centre development is due to be completed in 1980 in Cardiff, where as usual the 'home-work' has been painstaking and meticulous. In Britain Heron has been so selective that some ninety-five per cent of its rental income (from a total U.K. property portfolio of £65 million) comes from government utilities, insurance companies and major retailers. Sales of Suzuki motorcycles are flourishing — Britain being the only country where Suzuki sales are second only to Honda. Twenty-two service stations were opened between 1978 and 1979, and the Group now sells a hundred million gallons a year from major sites. Marketing efforts to keep up this gallonage are a non-stop process; offers and prizes have included a holiday in the U.S. flying by Concorde, helicopter trips to the Grand National and a car given away each month, as well as five pounds off a suit or a holiday, cut-price dry cleaning and restaurant meals, and even subsidised betting. These offers have been made possible by special arrangements with Ladbrokes, Willerbys, Sketchley, Avis and Heneky Inns.

The business philosophies which lie behind this vast and

growing organisation are clear and simple. Ronson sets the example of hard work, and his belief in it is demonstrated by the words written on a card which rests on Ronson's desk:

Press on
Nothing in the world can take the place of
persistence.
Talent will not; nothing is more common than
unsuccessful men with talent.
Genius will not; unrewarded genius is almost
a proverb.
Education will not; the world is full of
educated derelicts.
Persistence and determination alone are
omnipotent.

"He is extremely shrewd", one of his colleagues was quoted as saying: "he has an infinite capacity for hard work. He is one of the few men I've known prepared to invest money in ideas, and with the courage to take on the chore of running the operation to prove his belief in its potential" – an acknowledgement of Ronson's own precept of 'leading from the front'. Ronson in turn speaks generously of the contribution made by his fellow directors, many of whom have been with him for twenty years, but makes no bones about his own position. All major decisions pass across his desk, though he says they have all been unanimously agreed before they are taken. "But *I* am the architect of the team; I have built it up around me. Twice I have been tempted towards mergers, when I liked the people concerned, the business and the turnover. But we – in fact both sides – saw the light before the deals were consummated. We have our own identity and I am not sure how we would fare if we were amalgamated. While we are independent, we can be individuals in our own way; I am the Chief Executive here and can weld the whole thing together. I don't know how it would operate if we were part of a huge company".

From their beginnings in Chiswell Street with just one secretary, the Corporation has grown to its present huge size, employing nearly 6,000 people in Britain and overseas. Ronson knows many of his employees by name — the result of 70,000 miles a year travelling round his business — and does not want to grow beyond 10,000 employees in this country. "We couldn't run the business in the same style if there were more than that; there just aren't enough hours in the day. We are emphatically *not* a vast holding company; management and control are necessary to our style of running things, and must remain so. My management team is very able, very dynamic. They have dedication — Heron is their way of life. They have persistence and a capacity for hard work. There aren't any geniuses, but a lot of hard working honest people". Sometimes, Ronson admits, he wonders what makes them keep their heads down and get on with the job, hedged about as they are by bureaucracy and government controls, like all businesses, large and small. "I hope to see an improvement under Margaret Thatcher" he adds grimly.

The powerful self discipline which Ronson displays — dating back to his youth, when he desperately wanted to prove himself worthy of his father's trust and confidence — makes him an exacting boss. *"If there's no discipline, there's no business"* he maintains, and says that he himself is "hard, demanding, with very high standards. I'm really aggrieved if I find things are being covered up". On the other hand he realises the absolute necessity of being approachable. "I'm never too busy to listen and to help. If I don't care, how can I expect them to care? The problem in most big businesses is this; how can you expect the man on the shop floor to work hard when the managing director doesn't do the same? It's a lack of communication, when bosses haven't grown up with their men; you must have the touch, not a feeling of 'them and us'. I want the people who work for me to feel part of something; a successful company they can attach themselves to — job satisfaction if you like. Money is reasonably important of course, but people have got to be happy, to enjoy what they are doing". He cites Jules Thorn, founder of the well-known Thorn Electrical Industries, as an example of what he means — "he worked that way, built things up, knew the people and cared about them and what they were doing".

On the subject of education, Ronson is characteristically crisp. "Business schools, Harvard, Oxford, they're good. But what they cannot do is give you the feeling of being thrown in, say to an engineering company. You can't get the grass roots feeling from a business education, however good — not the feeling you get just by standing in the doorway of a firm, whether it's retailing or making nuts and bolts. You can tell almost immediately if the atmosphere is O.K. — ask a few simple questions, and experience tells you if all is well. You can't get that experience from a business school". He is grateful for the early discipline he experienced as a lad in his father's furniture factory, and regrets that people rarely have that sort of rigorous training today. "If you have a guv'nor growing up with the men, in their thirties, forties and fifties, you can have the best type of working relationship. It develops into general management. And the British working man is as good as any if he's motivated. If the guv'nor is only working from 9.30 to 4.30 these men don't feel they can relate".

Gerald Ronson cutting his fortieth birthday cake; specially designed and commissioned by friends and colleagues.

Looking back over his years with Heron, Ronson smiles. "It could hardly have been a worse time to be in the businesses we have been in! Many housebuilders went out of business, motor distributors were hit by the oil crisis in 1974/5, and then the property crash — to be in just one of them would have been bad enough, but to be in all . . ." But going through that period we were young enough and flexible enough to adapt, plus the leverage of our strong cash flow from the petrol stations. It's all been part of the maturing of the Corporation, and it's certainly made my co-directors twice the men today. They are lucky too, to have been able to grow with the business — so many reach a certain level and are incapable of making the next stage, but they have all been big enough to grow with it. When an entrepreneur looks at his mature company he can see how management has changed, how sophisticated it has had to become — you don't stop there. You can always go on, see possibilities of further improvement in performance and the quality of the people. If you are critical though, you've got to be critical constructively".

What is his attitude to risk? "You've got to take risks, of course, that's what business is all about". He has made some mistakes, inevitably, and admits to a few sleepless nights, but "as time goes on, one makes more and more of the right decisions". His own particular businesses are not for the fainthearted or those easily discouraged. "You cannot flap and you cannot show nervousness. It's no good looking terrified when the shells are coming at you! A few years ago it was pretty rough, as you may imagine, Rolls Royce bankrupt, the stock market at 150, interest rates at 17 per cent for gilt-edged securities. Some of the biggest names in the financial world were in difficulties. There we were, sailing the Atlantic in a force ten gale with ships sinking all round us. We weren't laughing, but we did keep our hands on the wheel and our eyes open. Your team will be O.K. if you are, and if you don't run away — I know, I've been there".

"And we still are here" he continues. "We didn't run away, and we didn't shirk our responsibilities. We sold some of our properties, certainly, but without loss, and we've kept the jewels in our crown — the rue de la Paix in Paris and Castellana in Madrid — they are landmarks in their own particular cities".

"As for the future — the world is getting smaller and capitalism is decreasing, while socialism and communism are on the increase. If you are a capitalist running a serious business — and I regard myself as a capitalist with a social conscience — then you must spread your eggs intelligently round a number of baskets. That's why I am concentrating now on the expansion of the respective divisions — just with the U.K. consumer business we've got enough to keep us busy for the next five years. There should be opportunities for a good wholesale business, for example, to operate in synergy with the rest of the Corporation. We'll find it and build it up — the best business is what you develop yourself".

KEITH WICKENDEN
Champion of Free Enterprise

Keith Wickenden is the Chairman of European Ferries —
described by the Daily Mail as Britain's most successful
shipping company. European Ferries is a holding company
whose eleven subsidiaries include the Townsend and Thoresen Car Ferries companies — marketed together with Atlantic
Steam Navigation Co. Ltd. under the name Townsend Thoresen — the Felixstowe Dock and Railway company, the
largest and most successful private enterprise port in Britain,
and a flourishing construction and property developing
division. All 'blue chip' operations in notably difficult
markets, adding up to a hefty £25.87 million in pre-tax
profits for 1978.

The belief in free enterprise which is the hallmark of
the group, (eight of its ships are called by that name, plus
an identifying numeral) was its mainspring from the start.
Taking a car to the Continent was an exasperating business
in the 1920s; it had to be winched on board and off again by
crane, with much consequent delay, and often damage.
Another source of grievance to drivers at that time was that
the Southern Railways on whose cross-channel mailboats
cars were transported, insisted on fuel tanks being drained,
but refused to compensate for the consequent loss of petrol.
A British artillery officer, Captain Stuart Townsend, was
infuriated on one occasion when his car was badly knocked
about while being onloaded, and he could get no redress, so

he and his brother decided to cock a snook at the established shipping services by chartering from her Tyneside owners the *Artificer*, an old collier which was carefully scrubbed out and found to be capable of carrying fifteen cars, (but only twelve passengers) and the first cross-channel ferry company aimed specifically at holiday motorists got under way in 1928, crossing from Dover to Calais, the fare undercutting the Southern Railways charges.

Business flourished and the brothers next bought a mine-sweeper, the *Ford*, which they re-named the *Forde*; she could take thirty cars, and was not replaced until 1950 when the former frigate *Halladale* came into service. Meanwhile, Southern Railways fought back in 1931 by introducing a custom-built car ferry, the *Autocarrier*, and Belgian Marine also began to offer a service to cars and passengers.

When business started up again after the six-year halt imposed by World War II, Townsends were still only operating one ship, but decided to go public by 1956, and actually did so on 26th July — the day Nasser seized the Suez Canal. However, the excitement on the international scene did not distract the attention of potential shareholders, and a controlling interest was soon acquired by a consortium of Midlands engineering companies based in Coventry, primarily Monument Securities, who were able to pick up the shares at minimal cost because of the timing. One of the Directors of the consortium was Roland Wickenden, brother of Keith, and like him, a qualified chartered accountant.

Wickenden had spotted the enormous potential of the car ferry market, and at the time the consortium took over the administration in 1957, Townsend was carrying 15,000 cars and 50,000 passengers annually, but within four years these figures had almost doubled. A new ship was ordered and came into service in 1962, named the *Free Enterprise*, and the headquarters moved south from Coventry to Dover. Roland Wickenden became firstly Managing Director of the shipping side, and then later took over as Chairman and Managing Director of the group.

1965 was an eventful year for European Ferries. They took delivery of another new ship, the *Free Enterprise II*, and started carrying commercial vehicles from Dover to

Calais; this traffic now accounts for about half of the over-all revenue of the company, and is carried on the four pur-pose-built European class freighters and other freight-carrying vessels as well as on the multi-purpose ships which make up the rest of the fleet. The following year, 1966, they estab-lished a route to Belgium, using the port of Zeebrugge, which now stands alongside the original Calais route in importance and volume of freight traffic.

By this stage the company was ready to start the planned series of acquisitions which have made a solid contribution to its growth and expansion. An obvious one was the Nor-wegian owned Thoresen company, which began operating in Britain in 1964, running a new car ferry service between Southampton and Cherbourg, and re-opening the Southamp-ton-Le Havre line previously abandoned by British Rail. European Ferries bought Thoresen in 1968, and thereby increased the fleet by three passenger car ferries and a roll-on/roll-off freight ship. Three years later they acquired the Atlantic Steam Navigation company from the government, to operate under the Townsend Thoresen umbrella, giving them six more ships (two of which have since been sold) and − what was to prove of significant future importance − routes from Felixstowe and across the Irish Sea from the Port of Cairnryan in Scotland.

In the few years since going public, the company had now progressed from operating one ship to owning or oper-ating (some of the Atlantic Steam Navigation vessels were on charter) a fleet of more than thirty. Its profits were rising handsomely too, but in October 1972 it was struck a tragic blow, when Roland Wickenden, returning through Belgium from launching a new ship in Holland, suffered a heart attack, and died at the age of 46.

Roland's family, and those working with him, were cer-tain he had contributed to this early death by sheer volume of work coupled with a meticulous attention to detail, without which, however, the group could never have achieved its overwhelming success; in the five years of his Chairman-ship for example, profits had jumped by an astonishing 1,700 per cent. He is described by former colleagues as a pleasant man, a shrewd and tough negotiator, though basi-

95

cally shy and happier when the limelight was switched off. Now, apart from the grief and shock attending his sudden death, there was a question mark over the fortunes of the company, which was seen in the City and elsewhere, as Roland Wickenden's creation. "A ship without a rudder", was how the *Financial Times* described it in the ensuing weeks — although this was an exaggeration. Kenneth Siddle, the current Managing Director, had been appointed to the Board some nine months earlier, as it was felt the firm was getting too big for one man to run virtually single-handed, so he took over immediately as Acting Managing Director. He too, however, although exceptionally capable, had always been the sort to eschew the limelight, and was relatively unknown to the City which, then as now, dearly loves a 'name' at the head of a big and prospering company of which it has great expectations. The share price plummeted, but the company had to keep going, ships had to keep sailing, and the Directors knew they had to be seen to be taking some action to re-assure the City, by appointing a new chairman. The action was to offer the chairmanship to Roland Wickenden's younger brother, Keith.

Like Roland, Keith is a qualified chartered accountant. Both had followed this path at the wish of their late father, who had started work in the office of a grain merchant directly he left school, displaying such numeracy that the firm's auditors had after some years offered him articles — almost unheard of at that time, when the fees for articles were considerable. Married by then, with a young family, he had been unable to take up the offer, but had always felt the loss deeply, and so encouraged two of his sons to follow this career. Roland had genuinely wanted to become an accountant but Keith calls himself one "by training rather than by inclination". He did his National Service in the R.A.F. — he is a qualified pilot — and wanted to stay in, but his father talked him out of it, saying there was no future in the Services in peace time, with which Wickenden now agrees. A further ambition was to play the saxophone in a dance band; he loves music and is very knowledgeable about it, playing the piano as well as the saxophone. He agreed to qualify as an accountant, but cherished a secret determination to start playing in a

Kenneth Siddle, Managing Director of European Ferries Ltd. since December 1972

band as soon as he finished his exams. However, when it came to the point, he opted for a more conventional career, and having taken his articles with a small firm in his home town of East Grinstead, he joined a slightly larger one in the Midlands, called Morris Dadley & Co.

Soon after he joined them, Morris Dadley merged with a Leicester-based partnership, Thornton Baker, and the new firm in turn bought up a small practice in Nuneaton where Wickenden went, to run what was in effect a branch office, acting as a 'local partner', who shared in the profits of his own office, but not in those of the whole firm. In 1959 he became a full partner and returned to Leicester where he stayed for three years, dealing with the affairs of clients mainly engaged in the engineering industry, many of them being sub-contractors to the motor trade — a considerable change from the farmers and small shopkeepers whose books he had audited during his articles in Sussex. It was "quite a large practice, but not by London standards, and I wanted to get back to London, which is after all, the centre of the accounting world.

There were no openings in Thornton Baker's London office, so at the end of 1962 he took the opportunity of returning south when the firm offered him a job in Horsham where he stayed for five years. He started specialising, almost by chance, in trouble-shooting jobs, for which he soon displayed great aptitude — an early example was the fraud case involving the State Building Society. The man responsible was convicted and went to prison, facing on his release, a total of forty-eight civil legal actions, in which Wickenden acted for the litigants, "almost living in Counsel's chambers for a year", and appearing as 'expert witness' for the plaintiffs. Other cases, as he began to take on more and more legal actions involving accountancy, included libel actions against newspapers, and one side effect of this experience was that he seriously thought of reading for the Bar, as he became more and more fascinated and involved with various aspects of the law. It came to nothing, because he realised he would have had to resign from the Institute of Chartered Accountants; just as practising as a solicitor disqualifies you from becoming a student barrister, so does practice as an accountant. Also, like his father, Wickenden was by then married with a young family, and could not afford to give up his accountancy work. However, at a later stage in his career, a similar involvement in something outside his immediate professional environment — this time the House of Commons — did lead him to extend his horizons outside his working life.

In 1968 he finally achieved his ambition of a place in Thornton Baker's London office in the West End, and "never having been very keen on audits — the bread and butter of accountancy", began to specialise in tax work, which he really enjoyed; "I liked the battle, the sense of fighting, the negotiation". An increasing part of his practice was the number of receiverships and bankruptcies in which he became professionally concerned, and these he enjoyed because of what he calls the "positive aspects". Occasionally, when a bank had appointed Thornton Baker as receivers, it became evident that the apparently doomed firm could be saved. "I really did like this, because so often in accountancy you are just commenting on decisions made by other people, rather than making your own". One example of a satisfactory turn-round, was the Rudgwick Clay Works, which had gone into receivership owing hundreds of thousands of pounds, and never had made a profit. It became clear to Wickenden that the root causes of the trouble were basically poor machinery, and lack of production. If one brick jammed the works, there could be fifteen men standing idle, waiting for the blockage to be cleared and any necessary repairs made to the plant. The owners had also failed to recognise, or at least acknowledge, that a special facing brick they made was in great demand in the building trade; so, instead of charging accordingly, they had priced it not much above the cost of an ordinary brick. Once these and other problems were ironed out, the debts were repaid, and within four or five years the receivers were able to hand back the company to its owners on a sound financial footing.

More spectacularly, Wickenden had been appointed one of the receivers to Rolls Royce after its notorious crash into bankruptcy in 1971, and this brought him to the attention of the City. Added to this, Thornton Baker was the

firm of auditors for European Ferries – dating back to the
Monument Industries consortium days in Coventry – and
what was more to the point, in the closing months of 1972,
Keith Wickenden, although not directly associated with his
brother's business, had been close to him, and familiar with
its broad outlines. "My brother used to discuss the business
with me as it grew – used me as something of a sounding
board, bounced ideas off me as it were. I was really the
only outsider to whom he could talk about it". Some years
earlier, Roland had actually offered him a job, but he turned
it down – "not because of any disagreement, we hardly
ever had any, but because I didn't want to go on being his
Number Two for the rest of my life".

Now the offer of the Chairmanship caused him "considerable heart searching – I didn't really want to accept it –
but eventually I did agree. I think it's fair to say that the
whole thing was viewed with some scepticism by the City –
they wondered if it was nepotism, and they would, I am
sure, have preferred a 'big name' even if it had not been on a
full-time basis". It would be interesting, if not particularly
relevant, to know if a brother has ever taken over, in similar
circumstances, a large and non-family firm. What is relevant
is that the sceptics were soon convinced that their investments were as safe as they had ever been in Roland Wickenden's day.

While very like his late brother to look at – colleagues
found the resemblance almost uncanny at first – Keith
Wickenden is by all accounts distinctly different in character. His love of battle, flair for publicity and palpable en-
joyment of public life, are in contrast to the quieter style
of Roland, and indeed to that of Ken Siddle. The younger
brother has a markedly puckish sense of humour too, and
none of this has done him, or European Ferries, anything
but good. This was indicated from the word go in his Chairmanship. One of his first commitments, within three weeks
of taking over, was to chair the Annual General Meeting,
and an A.G.M. of European Ferries is a lively affair. Shareholders, who increase in number each year take a genuine
interest in their company, and several hundreds of them
attend the A.G.M., unlike the usually colourless affairs

of most public companies, for which few bother to turn up, unless there is a likely looking scandal in the offing.

This particular meeting was an outstanding success, although Wickenden dismisses any question of personal triumph by remarking that "people were very kind, as they are in such circumstances". They had one special reason for congratulation, even though many of those present were probably unaware of the background. Shortly before Christmas, realising the cross channel ferry market was likely to expand smartly in 1974, (it did) European Ferries' marine architect, (now Technical Director) Jimmy Ayers and the Managing Director of the Dover operations, John Briggs, had found that a shipyard in Alblasserdam, upriver from Rotterdam, had a spare berth, and could build them a fourth new ship — three were already on order in Denmark. Should they go ahead and order it, they asked the new Chairman; the decision had to be made by January. "Give me Christmas to think it over", was the reply — and at the A.G.M. it was duly announced and warmly welcomed. This had a particularly amusing repercussion some years later. When Wickenden, along with European Ferries' main competitor in the private sector, and with the nationalised industry in the form of British Rail, was asked to give evidence before a Select Committee in the House of Commons on the subject of nationalisation, each was asked how long it took to decide to build a new ship, once the need had been identified. Nine months, said British Rail, and the private company said they took two months. Wickenden's reply was, "seven days if there's a Bank Holiday in between", which was greeted, he says, with disbelief, although perfectly true.

At this stage, although expanding rapidly, European Ferries was still a tightly-run operation, although the days of 'benevolent dictatorship' by the elder brother were bound to come to an end soon, if only because of the increase in size. Dover was still of overwhelming importance to the group, Southampton less so, and the routes to Felixstowe were operating successfully, but no particular steps had been taken to integrate that harbour into the overall scheme. "We had to set up a more formal management structure", says Wickenden, allowing that at the time it was "informal almost to the point of absurdity". One innovation was operational subsidiary boards, although "we are not a great board meeting company; in the seven years I've been here we've never taken a vote on the main board, a concensus has always emerged". A strong senior management team has been built up in the years since then, and Wickenden has frequently paid public tribute to their efficiency and, particularly, to their loyalty to the company. This is instanced by the fact that one of the directors was recently approached and offered four times his current salary by a firm of head hunters – the offer was declined.

Two further decisions taken within a short space of time proved "one right, one wrong". The right one was to buy Larne Harbour in Northern Ireland, for which European Ferries paid £1.3 million in 1973 – their first venture into the business of harbour operation. It has made a significant, and increasing contribution to group profit and fully bears out Wickenden's often stated belief in the value of short sea crossings, (the passage between Larne Harbour and Cairnryan is the shortest between Britain and Ireland) especially where, as here, they have introduced the speedy roll-on/roll-off freight services. Since road hauliers have heavy overheads in the shape of increasingly expensive vehicles, drivers' wages and insurance, they like to see their goods on the move on the roads, rather than incurring longer hours and charges at sea; and the expansion of Larne has been such that, while British Rail were providing three daily sailings each way, via Sealink, at the time of purchase, there are now over twenty. The shorter the journey, the more money the shipping company makes by increased volume of traffic, Wickenden emphasises. Larne has been such a success that it now handles 1.25 million passengers a year, and 60 per cent of the amount of dry (i.e. non-oil) cargo taken by Southampton. "An interesting port", remarks Wickenden, which has benefited from the many continental businesses which have set up in Northern Ireland.

The other decision was a less happy one, and was part of an unlucky chapter in the group's history. This was the acquisition of Invicta International Airlines. It was in financial difficulty at the time, and Wickenden and his fellow directors believed they could rescue it. Invicta was a cargo airline, carrying freight to Cyprus, Israel and Egypt, and other Middle Eastern destinations, as well as some passenger charter work, with a total of five aircraft and a history of twenty years flying with an excellent safety record. Only eight days after its purchase by European Ferries, a Vanguard on charter from Invicta, call sign 'Oscar Papa', crashed into a mountainside near Basle in Switzerland, killing more than one hundred people, most of them women from four villages in Somerset going on a shopping trip arranged by various clubs. This was in April 1973, in a period of extremely bad weather, but the crash has never been satisfactorily explained, and has become something of a classic aviation mystery — one recent theory being that the pilot was receiving signals from some disused pieces of telecommunication equipment formerly employed to send signals along parts of the French railway system — signals which had also been reported by other pilots in the vicinity. Miraculously, nearly a third of the passengers survived.

Further bad luck was to follow. A contract signed to carry oranges from Israel was just starting to operate, when the Yom Kippur war in October 1973 dried up the market overnight; another carrying grapes from Cyprus was similarly negated by the war against Turkey which broke out in July 1974. "We had had enough, and we closed it down", says Wickenden succinctly, adding that it taught the group an important lesson, and one they have carefully observed ever since; "we should stay in a similar type of business to the one we are doing, and in which we are experienced. We thought the airline business was similar, but in fact it's very different". In particular, they had failed to gauge just how much surplus capacity there was in the airline business, and the tremendous losses incurred as soon as anything goes wrong.

By 1973, the report of the Cross Channel Transport Improvement Council was able to note that European Ferries was "the only cross channel operator making an acceptable return on the value of its capital outlay"; and the capital outlay in question was becoming formidable.

103

No less than eight ships were launched in the two years following; 1974 and 1975; the first being the *Free Enterprise VIII*. There were also four of the 6,386 ton Super Viking Class, which were the biggest cross-channel car ferries ever built, and three European Class freight ships bought to make the most of the increasing importance of this trade (a fourth was delivered in May 1978). Also in 1974 a new service was established between Felixstowe and Zeebrugge,

Townsend Thoresen's Free Enterprise fleet carries cars and passengers from Dover to Calais and Zeebrugge.

which offered a convenient (and short) crossing from the north and east of Britain, as well as London. European Ferries have avoided sailing into Boulogne since their one trial period in the early 1970s, as it is not so well suited geographically to their operations.

All this activity was extremely important to the future of the group, but the story which was to capture the imagination of the British people was only just beginning to warm up; this was the battle for the port of Felixstowe.

The history of Felixstowe as a port goes back to 1875, when a local land-owner and engineer, called Colonel Tomline. had the necessary bill passed through Parliament to establish the Felixstowe Railway and Pier Company, and a thirteen-mile length of railway was built to link the Suffolk town to Ipswich; this was subsequently found unprofitable and sold off. Colonel Tomline, undaunted, set about his next enterprise, the Felixstowe Dock and Railway Company, which is still officially known by that name today, although generally referred to as the Port of Felixstowe. The company was floated in 1879, and the port was open for business by 1886, operating from two small wooden piers. The early years of this century saw a good deal of grain trade, which generated the money for a flour mill, grain silo and a new quay; and a maltings was also built to brew the barley grown throughout East Anglia.

By the outbreak of World War I, Felixstowe was large enough to be used as a Royal Navy base for destroyers and minesweepers, and in the next war it was taken over by the Admiralty, and used for motor torpedo boats. However, commercial traffic declined between the wars, and in 1951 the dock was sold to H. Gordon Parker, a Norfolk grain owner, popularly known as the 'father of Felixstowe port'. It was badly hit by the floods of 1953, but Parker doggedly set about improving the facilities, building new warehouses and mechanizing cargo handling operations by introducing new cranes and forklift trucks, which helped to speed up ship turn-round timings. By 1958 there was a Customs and Excise Landing Officer on the port, and the subsequent arrival of the Transport Ferry Service was another turning point. They had been pioneers of the roll-on/roll-off method of freight handling, and operated between Felixstowe and Europort at Rotterdam, as well as the Townsend Thoresen sailings to Zeebrugge mentioned earlier.

In 1973 European Ferries, alive to the possibilities of owning Felixstowe, then the only major non-nationalised port in Britain, had what Wickenden refers to as "a chat with their directors". By now they were gaining valuable (and profitable) experience from their simultaneous operation of Larne, and Cairnryan which had accrued to them (somewhat to their surprise), as part of the Atlantic Steam Navigation package: but the directors of Felixstowe opted for their independence, (Gordon Parker still in charge) and Wickenden and his board decided against pursuing them aggressively. However, at the Labour Party conference two years later, it was announced that British Transport Docks Board had come to an agreement with the directors of Felixstowe to acquire the port. "This really astonished us", comments Wickenden; "they were very anti-nationalisation, militantly free enterprise in fact; the port was often referred to as the jewel of free enterprise".

The shareholders accepted a 150p share cash offer (which put the value of the company at £5.24 million) from the B.T.D.B., and the next step was the necessary Private Bill to pass the ownership to the State. "We stepped in and made a bid over the heads of the directors, to the shareholders", explains Wickenden. This offer, coming two months after that of the B.T.D.B., was made in two stages, the second one proving to be the deal the shareholders were unable to resist, and which had 81.2 per cent acceptance by the middle of March, 1976. It put a higher value on the company — £6.8 million — and had only a small cash content, since it was a five-for-two share exchange offer, mischieveously 'baited' by European Ferries with an extra cash bonus of 15p per share *if* the Bill failed on its way through Parliament.

The stage was now set for an epic battle; and Wickenden had already shown a taste for such fights in his intervention in the Channel Tunnel dispute, when he had greatly enjoyed trumping official estimates and figures with his own, which he disarmingly owned later to be "entirely spurious, from the back of my head". The threat of nationalisation of Felixstowe, however, was far more immediate than the prospect of the Channel Tunnel actually carrying traffic, and it was clear that Wickenden with the now considerable weight of the ferry company, was not going to give in easily.

In the event, the fray lasted for another seven months after European Ferries' share offer. Inevitably, the press saw this, the first ever take-over battle with the government on one hand and a private company on the other, as a story in the David and Goliath mould, and it soon moved out of the financial sections of the newspapers onto the front pages. For European Ferries, there was a lot at stake. They were the main operators at Felixstowe, which had even in the current trading recession managed to return improved profit figures. The Port Users' Association was solidly on their side because the firm commanded considerable respect among its fellow 'short sea operators', and realised that despite the inevitable brouhaha of publicity, European Ferries were extremely experienced operators and skilful managers. The local landowners, Trinity College, Cambridge, backed them too, and they could point to their successes at Larne and Cairnryan, where profits had trebled and the number of dockers increased by some forty per cent in the previous three years. Labour relations were excellent at Felixstowe, (Wickenden felt that too many ports failed just because they were under-rated as investments, and dockers were under-rated as people) and the port was ideally situated for both freight and passenger traffic − offering access to many of the major trading routes linking the U.K. with North and Central America, North and West Africa, the Middle East and Europe. By 1975 it was handling 4.5 million tons of cargo − an increase of four million in only ten years.

Aerial view of the Port of Felixstowe.

Wickenden and his fellow directors "in our innocence", as he says now, had thought the Parliamentary Bill would be dropped once their bid was accepted, but there was no question of that, and "we went on to lose every battle except the last one". They tried unsuccessfully to get the Bill repealed on legal grounds; however, it was passed through the Commons — the justification from the B.T.D.B. being on the somewhat flimsy grounds that, "it could be disadvantageous for other users" if the chief user of the port owned it, (although the other users had dismissed this themselves, as already mentioned) and that it had no great experience of port operation. This was demonstrably untrue. The Bill was finally thrown out on its third reading in the House of Lords. "On Friday afternoon, October 22nd, 1976" remarks Wickenden with satisfaction, "the port was, and is, ours".

They are still under no illusion, he adds, that a Labour government, with a big majority, would not try to nationalise it. But he has often said that in this case, he would kick up such a row as would make the 1976 battle look like a storm in a teacup. He had had a room at Felixstowe at one stage of his R.A.F. National Service days, and "I'll fight like hell for Felixstowe".

This affair had an interesting spin-off as he became increasingly fascinated with parliamentary procedure, and this combined with his pessimism as he saw the country moving towards what he felt to be a real danger of Marxism. The upshot was that he was put on the Conservative Central Office's list of candidates in 1976, and in the 1979 election fought the safe Tory seat of Dorking, (near enough to his home not to have to move) winning with a majority of 19,763. Now he is a member of parliament, he says he is surprised to find he probably has more influence than he anticipated. "There are very few really, on either side, who have any business experience — particularly the Labour members. I do find I have something to offer; ministers come up and talk about business and ask questions". But he concedes that his parliamentary career poses something of a problem for him personally. If he got even a junior ministerial post (and he has been tipped as a possible Minister of Transport) he would have to give up his interest in European Ferries. "It's that or sit on the back benches for ever". At the moment, a few months after taking his seat, he is emphatic that his business career will take precedence. He needs his Euroferries salary, he points out matter-of-factly, and plans to spend his M.P.'s salary on a personal assistant to take some of the day-to-day parliamentary administration problems off his shoulders.

Though the 'battle for Felixstowe' looms large in the popular imagination, Wickenden, while speaking of it with justifiable pride, does not devote a great deal of time to its discussion, and there has been little time, and no inclination for those concerned to sit back and mull over past glories. Like successful generals, they have swept on to new ventures, (it is usually the lost battles which haunt one) and the increasing problems which success has paradoxically, brought them, and which has led to a very serious and thorough-going search for diversification. "The growth of the company over the next ten years is not governed by a search for finance, but how to invest our surplus funds", explains Wickenden.

Because of excess capacity in the shipbuilding business throughout the world, governments in the countries concerned offer generous terms to shipowners to build, including high loans as a percentage of cost, low interest rates, and long terms for repayment. (Incidentally, in Wickenden's estimation, "making the decision to build too easy. In the seventies many shipowners took too short a view, and bought ships from sheer joy of buying – to a certain extent creating their own difficulties"). In any case, by the time the Felixstowe affair was settled, the group had just come to the end of a period of heavy capital expenditure – £50 million in the previous two years – and by the end of 1976 was about to take delivery of its twenty-seventh ship, and complete the current shipbuilding programme. They had as many routes as they wanted, and were not sure they wished to expand their shipping interests. One area the group has concerned itself with, in an effort to deal with what could become an embarrassingly high rate of cash flow, and as a way of investing its money, is the property market; although the

Midas touch has operated here also and the company's involvement in this field has brought in some pretty hefty profits.

Links with the property business go back to the early sixties, when Roland Wickenden became interested in it, and they started up residential development on a small scale, mostly in the Midlands. Commercial developments were in parallel with the housing, such as a parade of shops in a housing estate. Keith Wickenden was not specially interested in this business, and when he took over he finished off what was under construction but, thinking the market was getting overheated, did not search out any new opportunities. So, by the beginning of 1973 European Ferries was more or less out of the market — and the following year the property bubble burst.

For three years or so, they kept away from it and then, when the slump seemed at its lowest point, and the secondary banks were disengaging themselves from property with as much haste as they had financed the boom only a few years before, European Ferries began to move into it again, "just when nobody else would touch it with a barge pole. But I always believe in going against the trend — we come in when others are going out". For this re-entry into the market, they started looking out for small office development sites in provincial towns, but nothing further north than the Midlands. Residential schemes were avoided, because both costing and pricing were too uncertain.

Characterised by what was described as 'extreme caution', the property dealings had one unusual feature. Having found a tenant or tenants after development, group policy — implemented by the Financial Services and Property Division — was to "dispose of the buildings to City institutions to hold as an investment. In many cases disposal arrangements have been concluded before building works commence", as Wickenden told his shareholders in his report for 1977. This is in direct contrast with the aims of most property companies, who tend to build up a 'portfolio' of investment and a cash flow derived from rental income.

Wickenden looks on property deals as "an arithmetical calculation", an attitude which may be calculated to provoke

110

those who prefer the general public, at least, to feel the whole area is full of mystique and needs a wide range of expertise. European Ferries calls on outside experts whenever necessary, and an increasingly important amount of its business is now carried on in conjunction with a property expert, Mike Bamber. Bamber is the Chairman of Brighton and Hove Albion Football Club, of which Wickenden, now a Director, became an ardent supporter, after years of little

Keith Wickenden and Mike Bamber watching Brighton and Hove Albion.

interest in the game, when he began taking one of his four sons to matches some years ago, and he enjoys flying himself to away matches.

The property deals are, predictably, getting larger and larger. The former Lyons Corner House site in the Strand was sold on, before work started, for a sum reported to be around £3.5 million, and central London figures largely in current plans in which Bamber and European Ferries are joint partners; shops and offices in Vauxhall Bridge Road, at Vauxhall Cross, Pickford's Wharf and in Old Burlington Street in the West End. The Vauxhall Bridge site has been subject to a series of exasperating planning delays lasting over two years. The site was bought from Land Securities for more than £400,000, and development of between £15 and £20 million is projected, including 100,000 square feet of residential property, and 20,000 square feet of shops, plus a 100 bed hotel. Construction of a riverside walk is also offered as a local amenity, but Lambeth Council has not, at the time of writing, been able to make up its mind to give the necessary go-ahead.

Townsend Thoresen Properties is a wholly-owned subsidiary, run by two managers who are both chartered surveyors and have a minority financial interest in the company. They concentrate on smaller provincial schemes as well as a few city centre 'plums' such as Enterprise House in High Holborn − near to the former Gamages site, being developed by another company, where rents of more than £15 per square foot have been rumoured. In Bournemouth, Townsend Thoresen's Morris House, 41,000 square feet, was financed by a pension fund, and let at £175,000 per annum to Abbey Life Assurance early in 1978.

Landlink Properties in Windsor was bought by the group in 1977 for about £1 million, and this deal increased the number of office sites for development. However, the biggest and most ambitious venture is the £750 million development in Denver, Colorado, announced early in 1979. In partnership with Vace Securities, a U.S. company, European Ferries is to develop a three hundred acre site, costing £16 million, in the city's flourishing Technological Centre, by means of a jointly owned firm called Tech Centre Developments. Five million square feet of lettings will include shops, housing and offices − in the middle of one of the most booming areas of the United States in the 'mile-high city'. European Ferries made what looks like a superb deal, putting up £125,000 of working capital, against Vace's £3.2 million and guaranteeing a £10 million loan from the Royal Bank of Canada who, along with N.W. Mutual Life, provided the finance. The British partner stands to receive

50 per cent of the profits from any land sales, and 40 per cent from any development sales. The potential over ten to fifteen years is very high and, as Wickenden has remarked, "the gearing is phenomenal". The speed of working in the U.S. makes delays like those at Vauxhall doubly aggravating. Wickenden notes admiringly that if you haven't received an answer to a planning application in Denver within four weeks, you can go ahead; he is also on record as saying that, although Americans are excellent property developers, they are relatively unsophisticated when it comes to finance.

They have made various other acquisitions in pursuit of diversification, of which the most substantial so far has been the purchase, also in 1977, of the English and Caledonian Investment Trust, paid for by an issue of ordinary shares. The Trust was valued at around £13.2 million, and the newly combined balance sheet showed investments of £18.8 million, and cash £13.2 million. This takeover of a cash-rich company helped to reduce the group's debt; equity ratio of less than 1 : 1 in spite of further extremely expensive capital investment plans (described later) at Larne and Felixstowe. Wickenden views the new subsidiary as a firm basis for further possible diversification in the financial world, perhaps buying up a ship broking firm (or firms) and insurance broking where, in spite of disappointments in the past, Wickenden is still looking for likely opportunities. It has not been easy for them to find the right kind of company; they are only in the market for finance based companies, and not interested in manufacturing. Nonetheless, the Financial Services and Property Division brought in nearly £5.5 million in profits in 1978, and can hardly fail to continue growing, although Wickenden knows he must make sure it does not become the dominant element in the group.

Some people, although Wickenden is self-evidently not one of them, find property *per se* enthralling and romantic. Many more will thrill to the idea of a new venture about which Wickenden himself is infectiously enthusiastic; airships. The Thermoskyship scheme was dreamt up by Malcolm Wren, an ex-major in the Royal Engineers. He approached European Ferries in 1974 for financial backing, and Wickenden and his fellow directors were sufficiently impressed by the outline scheme, to carry out studies on it, together with two other public companies; "but we had to give the thumbs-down – it was too ambitious. He was going for a 400-ton payload machine, about the size of the Oval cricket ground! – and we felt it was an unjustifiable risk". Wren worked on his designs with his brother, however, and came back in 1977 with a new plan which evoked more serious interest. This time the payload was a more realistic ten tons, with a hundred passengers. European Ferries agreed to pay £2 million, providing other support was forthcoming, towards the estimated total development cost of £6 million. It was to be built in the Isle of Man (good labour relations, and less danger of state take-over), and they would be the biggest shareholders, with an option on the first six models. "Some people are still taking it as a joke", says Wickenden, "but they are making a mistake".

Even those who do take them seriously, are often worried about the danger of airships bursting into flame. Wickenden points out that they had flown about 50 million flying miles, including a regular transatlantic service, over a period of twenty-seven years before anyone was killed, and the problem of inflammability has been solved by replacing the risky hydrogen with helium, "which just can't burn, even if you put a blow-torch to it". In fact the properties of helium are such that it could be used to fill up interstices in the skyships for safety purposes.

The Wren brothers made a first, successful flight in 1975 at R.A.F. Cardington and Wickenden expected the first production model (likely to cost around £1.8 million apiece) to be in scheduled service between European cities within the next three to four years. The skyships would carry mainly passengers, and are not designed for long distances. Flying at a height of about 2,000 feet at 100 mph, they will do the journey from London to Paris in two and a quarter hours with a following wind, at an estimated single fare of £20. "They are extremely comfortable", points out Wickenden (who says he would like to pilot the maiden voyage) "with bars, restaurants, duty free shops; space is no problem, and they could if necessary run on natural gas, there's room to carry it stored under pressure". There is no new technology involved, but engines and navigational aids are incomparably better than those available to the 'first generation', which came to a halt in 1938, when the Germans finally took the *Graf Zeppelin* out of passenger service. European Ferries is already looking out for suitable landing sites. Airships can hover, and land and take off vertically, like a helicopter, so it will theoretically be possible to travel city centre to city centre, and the dockland area of London is a distinct possibility. Wickenden envisages someone currently flying to Paris, leaving his office in London at least two hours before the flight is due, held up en route by congested roads, and arriving at the hideously overcrowded Heathrow. "On an airship he could have been in Paris before the aircraft takes off".

Tests in a computerised wind tunnel have shown the best shape for the new breed of skyship is a saucer, rather than the familiar cigar, as this gives improved handling capability. They have the added advantages of low noise and negligible air pollution, and other possibilities that have been mooted in addition to carrying passengers (they are probably not economic for freight) are for aerial crane work, anti-submarine warfare, fishery protection, electronic surveillance and work connected with off-shore oil and natural gas production.

Since my first meeting with Mr Wickenden, due to the lack of any outside financial support, this fascinating project has had to be shelved, and the company continues to concentrate on its bread and butter, the transport of freight and of passengers; each of which accounts for an almost equal volume of business. A former naval dockyard at Harwich has been added to their port ownership, while at both Larne, and particularly Felixstowe, there are great plans for expansion, totalling some £100 million, already under way. Larne has benefited from grants from the E.E.C. Regional Development fund, and Northern Ireland port modernisation allowances, to help finance its £3.5 million scheme, which includes the building of two-tier loading ramps, similar to those in operation at Felixstowe. The Suffolk port is engaged on a massive programme involving, at the first stage, the

Some of the passenger facilities in the new £1 million Townsend Thoresen terminal at Felixstowe.

expenditure of some £8 million between 1977 and 1979, most of which is earmarked for re-equipping the container handling division. The port's Managing Director, Geoffrey Parker, has estimated that during 1977 Felixstowe had to turn away about 200,000 box units of 'serious business', so at the end of that year it was decided to buy three transtainer rubber tyred gantries. Three more were subsequently ordered from Vickers, who have built all six machines in Britain, under licence from the Paceco Corporation of Almeda, California. This decision to switch over completely from the former conventional 'straddle' carrier fleet, was only taken after extensive simulation studies had shown the advisability of making such a change. The cost of the new transtainers and carrying out associated roadworks, plus installation of new Tugmasters and forklift trucks, will be over £6 million; part of the cost of a new rail-mounted gantry crane for the Freightliner terminal (£170,000 in all) was met by a grant from the Department of Transport.

Other innovations and modernisation at Felixstowe include a new £1 million passenger terminal (opened by Princess Anne in February, 1979), office blocks and ware-house space – one warehouse specifically for paper – all designed to increase container roll-on/roll-off trade by at least 40 per cent. More development is planned next to the northern extension, which was built up between 1972 and 1974; and a bridge over the River Orwell, plus a dual carriage-way Ipswich by-pass, are planned to be in use by the early 1980s. So there seems every possibility of Felixstowe be-coming, as Wickenden has forecast, Britain's premier dry, or non-oil, port within the next decade.

In 1977 the company ordered another European class freight ship, which entered service in May 1978, the 3,367 ton *European Enterprise*, which is based at Dover, and together with her sister ships, the *European Trader* and the *European Clearway*, plus seven Free Enterprise class ships, provides some fifty-eight sailings a day to Calais and Zee-brugge. When Wickenden announced in the course of 1978 that he was going to place orders for another batch of ships – three, as it turned out – he made it clear that the group hoped it would be possible to build them in British yards, though he warned that this would depend on price, delivery dates (of overwhelming importance to shipping companies who have to announce sailings and take bookings many months in advance), quality and commercial guarantees. He commented to his shareholders that he would be interested to learn whether the surprising terms offered to Polish shipowners by the British government would be available to a British shipowner.

Twenty-six yards were reportedly asked to tender for the three new multi-purpose ferries, but contrary to Wickenden's hopes, the British Shipbuilders' tender was the highest (an estimated 30 per cent above the German figure and 50 per cent above tenders from the Far East). Would-be shipbuilders were "knocking my door down", says Wickenden, who was disappointed that the intervention could not, apparently, be stretched to cover the difference between the U.K. and West

German bids. The three new ferries are being built at Bremer-haven at the Schichau shipyard of Unterweser A.G., (who built the group's other four freight ships) and will be in service by the end of 1980. European Ferries made another shrewd deal, paying in sterling with a government undertaking to underwrite any risk from fluctuations in the exchange rate.

To the general public — and some 40 million passengers cross the Channel in a year — Townsend Thoresen is the best known name in the group and this has been accomplished by

Viking Venturer, in Townsend Thoresen's luxury Super-Viking class, plying the company's routes from Southampton and Portsmouth to Le Havre and Cherbourg

an aggressive marketing policy, combined with a solidly based reputation for modern ships, comfortable service and the aforementioned access to ports equipped to handle traffic quickly and smoothly. There is not much room to compete in price levels, but the group has an imaginative programme geared to achieving its stated target of around 60 per cent of the market. Even today, only four per cent of car-owners in Britain take their vehicles abroad, leaving a huge potential market as yet untapped, and Townsend Thoresen in any case would not be able to sit still. Hovercraft operations are expected to increase sharply in the next few years, and competition from Sealink and the smaller P & O's Normandy Ferries is not under-rated by European Ferries. Sealink has been enlivened recently by a youthful and enthusiastic management team; in addition, two new berths at Dover are due to come into operation in 1980, which will add to the competition.

The multiplicty of Euroferries' routes has become evident in the course of this study, but it is undoubtedly an important element in their success. They have been similarly successful in increasing the number of shareholders by a series of imaginative 'perks'. Almost half the 92,000 shareholders in the company are private individuals, and holders of 300 or more shares get two cut-price trips a year, but this has brought some problems in its wake for the new computerised booking procedure installed at Dover.

A scheme announced in the summer of 1979 also created quite a stir — European Ferries linked up with Britain's only independent university college at Buckingham, to offer shareholders the unique opportunity of taking a degree course there. The firm has long been interested in the possibility of setting up company-funded scholarships, and the new plan is to finance a series of places at the University College of Buckingham, during the period January 1980 to December 1985, covering tuition, residential fees and books. They will be available to successful applicants, who must hold at least 1,000 shares in European Ferries dating from January 1st, 1977, plus anyone employed by the company from or before that date, and their close relations. Employees will receive normal salaries during the two- or three-year course, but must guarantee to stay with the company for two years after completing it, and cannot be graduates of any other university. "An innovative college welcomes this innovation by a company recognised as a leader in innovations", as it was put by the College at the time of the announcement.

New ideas for holidaymakers themselves are plentiful too.

Townsend Thoresen pride themselves on their on-board service, which embraces not only practical elements such as a bank on the ship for currency conversion, but extras in the form of feature-length film showings and special film programmes for children, 'fun fayres' with games of luck and skill, and a lucky dip, with prizes selected from the gift shops on board, and a free return trip the following year for a car and two passengers.

In March 1978, the company launched a service between Felixstowe and Rotterdam − the fifth new route in six years − and it also runs a holiday village, De Haan on the Belgian coast, only nine miles from Zeebrugge. They opened the Dover Motel on the A2 in November in conjunction with George Hammond & Co. Ltd. from Dover, at a cost of £750,000, conveniently near their Dover ferry terminal. Also, in spite of initial misgivings about the narrow profit margins, the group has expanded their package holidays in the last few seasons from short motor packages to a series of Townsend Thoresen coach tours. This was a rather unexpected venture, as Euroferries had previously avoided inclusive holiday schemes, not just on financial grounds, but because they were aware that the established tour operators were their customers, with whom it might prove unpopular to enter into competition. However, they have been careful to complement, rather than go into outright competition. For instance, not owning their own coaches, these are leased from the regular operators, thus augmenting their business. They have not gone into road haulage or freight business on their own account, ascribing part of their success in freight to the fact that their main competitors, P & O and British Rail, *are* in it.

However, Townsend Thoresen coach tours operated exclusively by Townsend Thoresen Holidays look like being as successful as their other innovations, and they have pre-empted criticism on the grounds of going into competition with their own clients, by operating their short package tours in conjunction with one of the largest specialist tour operators in the business, Anglo-World Travel of Bournemouth who are primarily concerned with running coach tours of Britain for incoming visitors to this country. They have always avoided long sea passages as they are uneconomical, but this does not preclude them operating routes inside other countries, and they have made satisfactory agreements with two established operators in Spain and Scandinavia to act as U.K. agents starting in 1979. The operators are Gedser-Travemunde Ruten A/S., who run services from north Germany to southern Sweden and Denmark, and Ybarra, the Spanish operator of the Barcelona-Palma, Majorca service.

European Ferries has managed to avoid the worst of the problems inherent in the seasonal nature of the cross channel operation from the U.K., (most routes from the south coast are only profitable, as regards passengers, in the brief summer school holiday period) by a judicious mixture of freight and car ferry work, and by carrying freight in the same ships as carry passengers, sometimes even on the same sailings if passenger bookings are low. Also, Townsend Thoresen has made a big effort to attract off-peak traffic, virtually creating the popular Saturday shopping trips to the Calais hyper-market just before Christmas – another example of innovation and attention to detail and customer convenience. They also had specially made Townsend Thoresen tents for campers, and when there were complaints that their camping equipment contained only one freezing block for use in the insulated picnic boxes, immediately increased them to two; one to go in the box, and one to return to the 'fridge for recharging. Sadly this camping operation has since been dropped. It is, however, this sort of thing which gives Townsend Thoresen, and the whole group, the edge over its main competitors. Likewise on the freight side, "you are a customer, and Townsend Thoresen wants your business", proclaim the brochures, offering expert help and advice through the daunting complexities of official regulations surrounding the movement of cargo from one country to another. One of Wickenden's principal qualities is that he "trusts people, and lets them get on with the job", as a colleague puts it. He has said he feels the almost obsessive personal attention to detail his brother gave to all aspects of the business had contributed to his early death, and Keith Wickenden is not going to let himself fall into a similar trap.

The astonishing growth of the company, which now

employs nearly 6,000 people, coupled with the vast number of its individual shareholders, does mean its continuing independence seems guaranteed. The Conservative victory in 1979, quite aside from the personal election of the Chairman as an M.P., has renewed its confidence in the future, and it is significant that the group increased its donation to Conservative party funds from £10,000 in 1977 to £15,000 the following year, entirely at the instigation of shareholders, fearful that a Labour election victory would spell the end of Felixstowe's independence. Almost the first move after the election was to announce talks being held to consider further major expansions there, such as dredging a deeper channel into the port. Wickenden has high hopes of less government interference in business under the new administration, "if only they'd sit back and leave us to get on with it!"

They have shown how they 'get on with it' in the troubled matter of labour relations. While dockers are viewed as traditionally militant, and the restrictive practices of unions in London have contributed to the decline of the docks there, hardly any serious disturbance occurs in the ports owned by European Ferries. This is partly due to their high pay, and Wickenden also observes that the port has inherited no "legacy of bitterness like there is in London, Liverpool and Southampton". Gordon Parker was an enlightened man, he was close to the men and communicated with them, he knew about their problems almost as soon as they appeared and could deal with them immediately. This tradition has been carried on by the present owners, and the Managing Director's door is always open, with shop stewards coming in and out. The port is so obviously prospering that it gives the men a sense of security; much militancy, Wickenden feels, is a direct result of the fear of losing one's job. The prosperity at Felixstowe is not confined to the port, but has also brought considerable security to Suffolk and the whole of East Anglia.

There is no centralised committee in European Ferries for handling labour relations, and Wickenden emphasises that each local unit deals directly with the unions concerned, on the spot. These are primarily three; seamen belong to the National Union of Seamen; officers to the Merchant Navy

Keith Wickenden enjoys farming on his seventy acre farm, when he has the time

and Airline Officers' Association; and the dockers to the Transport and General Workers' Union. Euroferries employees tend to work in relatively small groups, particularly on board ship, and this is an advantage; "they have the ear of someone if they have a grumble".

Would he recommend anyone today to go into shipping? "Yes, on the whole I think I would, on similar principles to what I said about the company going against a trend. In car ferry work especially, it's a good existence if the sea's in your blood — as it undoubtedly does get into people's blood — and yet allows you to lead a normal family life as well. The longest time you are likely to be away is one week on, followed by one week off, and you are back in port every few hours, so if something is wrong you can always get home for an hour or two".

Wickenden himself appears to have a fairly hectic family life, with his four lively sons, a seventy acre farm and 300 sheep, though he claims his wife is the "real farmer" in the family. He also keeps wicket for his village cricket team. No-one who spends even a short time with him can doubt what is in his blood — a belief in business, in value for the individual and even more for the country, and in its continuing independence and freedom. Captain Townsend, one feels, would wholeheartedly approve. And he would probably commend Wickenden's parting analysis of his own business methods: "avoid management consultants like the plague. Trust your own judgment. All management is common sense, and all business is the same, whether it's I.C.I. or a tobacconist on the corner. The principles are the same — it's just the size that's different". Coming from somebody who in the six years since he took over, has increased his company's profits from under £5 million to 25.8 million, that could be valuable advice.